A Certain Lack

One person's reflection on the human species and his improbable hope for a new age of reason

Written by Alex Buzzard

Acknowledgements

I would like to thank my wife Gaynor for her untiring support in the undertaking of this book, her patience putting up with the writer's mood swings throughout its creation, and her wise words of advice on style and content. I would also like to thank Bryan, Beth, and Debra for their help and advice after agreeing to read through the draft manuscript.

A special word of thanks to Debra Darling for her permission to use her artwork for the book's cover.

Table of Contents

A word of warning, this book may damage your faith

Before we start our journey together through these pages I feel I should first warn you that you will not find the truth within these pages. You will only find the perspectives of one who humbly tries to seek it, but who knows, alas, that this is a lifelong journey that will have no end.

One of the strangest absurdities expressed in the world of humanity is the universal misuse of the word truth. Alas, anyone who professes to speak the truth is somewhat lacking in self-reflection. We human beings don't know the truth. Human beings start their lives with the contents of their brains limited to the instinctive programming and emotional attachments inherent at the time of their birth. From this point onwards the human mind is continually augmented through life by the further gathering of information and experiences from the environment which the brain tries to interpret through the impulses of our senses.

When we humans express an opinion, unless deliberately lying, we are expressing what we believe to be true based on our attempts to process the limited information at our disposal in our mental databases and our instinctive programming. This is why arguments can be so much fun to observe as they usually start from the perspective that the participants all genuinely believe they are right. There is no shortage of humans prepared to stand up and tell others what they firmly believe the truth to be, but it is incumbent upon us all to use whatever cognitive abilities we have to put such claims to proper scrutiny. It is a sad characteristic of our species that all too often we fail to do this and in this vein I encourage readers to subject anything they may read in this book to the same rigorous test.

Everyone who goes to court and states that they will state the truth, the whole truth, and nothing but the truth should be immediately locked up for perjury and the court should hold itself in contempt for asking such an obviously absurd statement! The best that any human can be asked is to state what they perceive to be true at that moment in time, based on the information that has been made available to them and the limitations of their cognitive abilities.

Scientists amongst you will know this only too well. Yes the truth does exist, but this is only a conceptual idea and it would only be evident to us if we were blessed with universal knowledge. As humans we can but strive to refine our perceptions but let us relish this, after all we may never get to our desired destination but the journey can be awe inspiring and fun. Scientists work on the basis of the latest developed theory argued by submitting the evidence known to them at the time. They know that it is the destiny of many of these theories to be amended or discarded as new evidence comes to light.

What you will find within these pages is one person's perspective on the world as he sees it. This book will have achieved its limited objectives should it stimulate just one new line of thought in any reader kind enough to accompany me on a journey through its pages.

I feel that I have a duty to offer an advisory caution to a certain group of potential readers whose lives are guided by their attachment to religious faith. This is particular pertinent to those who are guided by their emotional attachment to a conception of God as described in the Old Testament. This book is intended as a dialogue with those humans who like me often feel like a "square peg in a round hole" when trying to observe the peculiar antics of our species from a rational perspective. Those of sincere faith, as opposed to those objectively seeking clues to help their understanding of the truth of things, will have already chosen to come to the end of their journey of self-enquiry. It is sadly not possible to mix the rigours of reasoned argument with the properties of a powerful emotional attachment to religious ideas and imagery. A mind that is open and receptive to new ideas is an essential prerequisite for any reasoned argument to have value to those engaged in the process. A rational evaluation of many religious texts reveal that they include numerous contradictions and are often confounded by subsequent overwhelming historical and scientific evidence. Both these aspects make a number of religious texts a legitimate subject for considerable re-evaluation and re-interpretation within this book.

Those firmly locked in their particular faith are hereby kindly invited to exercise their freedom of choice at this point and proceed no further into a book that will make arguments they may find quite uncomfortable and potentially a source of offense. I fully recognise that for many their faith is an important stabilising factor in their lives and a point of reassurance in an often chaotic world. I have no desire to be a source of further consternation or in any way influence those who have firmly taken this path in life. As an author, I am merely choosing to exercise my freedom to express my views. This freedom has rarely been as threatened as it is today, but is still claimed to be one of the most cherished rights of the particular, and often peculiar, society into which I was born and continue to live.

This book is intended for open and free minded spirits who share my concerns about the irrationalities manifest in the human world, and have common interest in exploring the possibility that there could be a new and more rational future for our species. Who knows, maybe you too will be inspired to start your own conversations and share your observations of our strange human world. I have a personal belief that a new age of reason is centuries overdue. Rather than evolving, humanity seems rather to be regressing towards ever increasing irrationality led by those who have vested interests in maintaining this dynamic. I firmly believe it is time for humanity to face up to the peculiar myths and legends that are still prevalent in many societies with often disturbing consequences. It is time for our species to evolve and start taking both personal and collective responsibility for shaping a more rational future and preserving our wonderful but fragile planet that is increasingly threatened by our collective actions.

Synopsis for the prospective reader: "so what's this book all about before I waste my valuable time and money on it?"

I think it is only fair to give any unsuspecting prospective reader an idea about what this book is aiming to convey so that they have an opportunity to escape from its clutches at their earliest convenience.

As stated in my well intentioned warning, this is my way of sharing with other members of our rather strange species my concerns about what I believe are some of the peculiarities inherent in humanity that are catastrophically inhibiting our ability to evolve as a species. I will argue that this barrier to evolution is not just manifest at an individual level but also in the institutions that influence our lives and societies and that consistently appear to fail the majority to the advantage of the few.

I will share my observations about a property which I describe as human attachment behaviour (HAB) and how I believe this dominates so much of our lives. I shall theorise about how such a potentially debilitating quality could actually have evolved as a successful evolutionary trait which, in the modern world so severely limits humanity's potential to build a more rational future for itself.

During these observations I shall draw on examples that best illustrate the strange properties of HAB. I shall look at religions and differentiate between those demanding blind faith and those that seek to evolve the human consciousness which I call the "wisdom traditions". I will argue during this analysis that one of the greatest travesties ever committed against our species was the hijacking of the teachings of a teacher in the "wisdom tradition" named Jesus. I will supply evidence that this unintended crime was misguidedly committed by early Christians through the creation of a tragic association of his teachings with the God of the Old Testament.

I will refer to texts from the Old Testament and the Qur'an in order to try to get a measure of the character they portray of God and make what I believe is a perfectly legitimate assertion that no rational mind could possibly wish to be associated with such an entity. I will discuss why the peculiar properties of HAB explain not only why so many humans do make such an attachment, but why it is virtually inevitable. I will argue that religious attachment very effectively illustrates HAB's incredible power and influence over the behaviour of humans. I shall also observe how effectively HAB is used by both religious hierarchies, and the rulers and politicians who continue to work hand in hand with them, to manipulate their fellow humans and legitimise their own personal agendas.

During my illustrative journey through the world of religion I will also draw upon the teachings of what I assert to be a "wisdom tradition". I believe the teachers in this tradition fully understood the potentially malevolent properties of HAB and conscientiously strived to help humanity to escape from its clutches. I will also theorise about why these worthy efforts, although having significant impact upon individuals who seek and strive to understand, have inevitably failed to have any significant impact upon the mass of humanity.

I shall explore some of the obvious absurdities of our attachments to extreme capitalism in a supposedly democratic western tradition and how HAB enables the capital addicts in our midst to exploit the system at the expense of their fellow humans. I will also argue that the very nature and existence of these extreme capitalists is an absurdity both to themselves and to wider society. During this analysis I will look at the very peculiar aspect of HAB that allows capital addicts to effectively associate their malevolent practices with the teaching of faith based religion (particularly evident in the USA). I will make an argument for the case that this contagious viral capitalism has become a religion of the modern age, and that it is only the peculiar properties of HAB that explains humanity's self-imposed slavery to a system that actively discriminates against the interests of the majority.

I will end the book with some concluding observations that in order to build a better and wiser world, humanity needs to recognise and accept its slavery to the properties of HAB. If we are not to re-enact the collapse of our financial systems in an age when literally trillions of dollars can move around the globe in a matter of seconds we need to build a new society based on mitigating HAB's more malign qualities. Indeed if our irrational slavery to HAB is accepted and objectively examined, I shall argue that its properties could actually be used positively to create a more equitable and rational future for our species and the other beings that share our World.

Well prospective readers, you have now been doubly warned and should you choose to continue, you do so at your own risk!

Chapter 1 – Human attachment behaviour (HAB) - our peculiar species and the attachments it makes in defiance of reason

Welcome to this conversation about the peculiar species living on the planet Earth that I shall refer to in the coming pages as humanity. This conversation about my species is the one that I dearly wished for when I was younger when I was trying to understand what seemed to me to be obvious absurdities and contradictions within human behaviour. These seemed quite apparent even as a child and yet none of the responsible adults to whom I related my feelings ever seemed to be able to come up with cohesive answers to my expressed concerns and observations. Most of the people I turned to did not even share my view that there was anything particularly strange about human behaviour and could not really understand why I should be so perplexed about such matters. This conversation is therefore not written for all of those members of humanity who feel at ease with human behaviour and the societies in which we live. It is written as a reassurance to others of my species, who may feel as alienated and isolated as I did when I was growing up. You are probably not going insane at all but are instead most likely to be suffering from the consequences of an alternative and, I would argue, unusually rational sense of the world about you. In short this conversation is my attempt to bring some comfort and hope that you are by no means alone and isolated. There are many others who feel, and have felt throughout the history of our species, the same way that you may be feeling now.

I have already posted an introductory disclaimer that this book does not claim to explain the truth as this is an unknown quantity to the human experience. It is merely a perspective from a fellow human trying to make sense of what he observes of the human world and make suggestions from this perspective as to how we might attempt to improve on the current model of human civilisation. The purpose is purely to provoke thought and discussion and to provide encouragement to fellow human beings who may have an inclination to join in the debate. During this book I have called on the help of a representative from another alien species, an outside rational being who has taken an interest in humanity and has the capacity to ask some very awkward questions about our species. I have shamelessly stolen the concept of this idea from G.I. Gurdjieff (Beelzebub's tales to his grandson) but I make no apology for this. The approach of using an external rational perspective provides a useful vehicle for looking at, and starkly questioning, the many aspects of humanity that are so firmly ingrained in our collective psyches. It also allows me to attempt to fool the otherwise discerning reader who may have some well-founded question marks about my sanity, that I am not just talking to myself!

Within this book I will refer to the views of the rational being accompanying me through these pages as ORB (my Outside Rational Being) and ask the reader to humour this flight of my imagination and to join me in looking at aspects of our behaviour from ORB's rather critical perspective.

ORB:- It's a pleasure to make your acquaintance

It is no easy task being human and therefore as a fellow sufferer of this affliction I empathise with you and the plight in which we find ourselves. It is truly an extraordinary challenge to tackle the limitations of our peculiar species, maybe impossible, but I believe that it is certainly worth having a bash at trying to suggest a more rational and sustainable future for the generations to come. I have pondered over many years about the often highly irrational attachments that humans make to objects, ideas, organisations and nationalities. Although I wrestled with this for much of my life I think this first became truly clear to me whilst I was at university when I was trying to think of a topic for my dissertation. I had this eureka moment in the shower and rushed downstairs in my towel, much to the alarm of the poor housemate in the kitchen at the time, shrieking "teddy bears!"

Even at an early age our minds start making attachments to the most improbable things. If we look at a teddy bear, both the child and the parents know that it is just a stuffed bag of material but the emotional attachments are none the less all too real. If anything should happen to Teddy there is genuine distress in the household. This is so familiar to us that we don't actually stop to think how strange a behaviour this is from any rational perspective.

I can remember around this time there was a terrible foot and mouth epidemic in the UK and literally hundreds of thousands of cattle were being culled. One paper took a picture of a calf that had somehow managed to survive, having been shielded by the dead bodies of other cattle from the attention of the people from the ministry. They named this calf Phoenix (as in the mythical bird that rises from the ashes) and put a picture of this pretty calf with eyelashes prominently in the newspaper.

The rules at the time were absolutely clear; Phoenix had to die as part of a suspect herd. However the public outrage, initiated by the attachment they had created with Phoenix through the extensive media coverage, reached such a level of intensity the ministry actually backed down and changed the rules. They undertook extensive tests on Phoenix which showed no actual infection and the calf's life was therefore spared. Almost instantaneously a very significant number of humans had created a very strong emotional attachment to this one animal whilst so many others continued to be culled. There was absolutely no rational reason to spare Phoenix more than any other animal but it was becoming apparent that I was not observing rational behaviour but something altogether more strange and powerful.

Another incident that vividly springs to mind was the public reaction to the death of Diana, Princess of Wales. The media at the time described a "field of flowers" outside Kensington Palace representing a wave of grieving from huge numbers of the public. A friend of mine living in London at the time said that the scent from so many blossoms was almost overpowering. Many people I met after Diana's untimely death were showing signs of personal distress and loss and appeared to be genuinely grieving. If we were to look at this rationally, rather than from a familiar emotional perspective, very few of those in grief had ever met Princess Diana or knew what she was really like as a person. These people had created a very real and powerful attachment to a personal something deep within their psyche that was intrinsically linked to their self-developed relationship with the Princess. In some very real and powerful sense they identified with this personal picture they had created of her within the recesses of their human psyches. The sense of emotional loss I perceived was therefore entirely genuine in most people.

Far less dramatic attachments can be seen in the relationships that people make with characters in fictional soap operas or with a football team. I could better understand these attachments to football teams if they represented the fan's area, and if the players were from the actual community where they lived. Further observation shows us that this is very far from the truth in most cases, particularly in relation to the teams playing at the highest levels. I can remember teasing an Arsenal fan who never lived in London and at a time just after the French manager, Arsène Wenger had been newly appointed. I think there was actually only one English player in the team. What is the rational link for my friend's continued devotion to a club for which he had no obvious association whatsoever? Despite this observation, my friend's attachment was extremely strong and I knew that if I continued in my jesting it would elicit increasing levels of irritability with me or even hostility. I equally instinctively knew that no amount of rational argument on my part would have made the slightest different to my friend's devotion. Whatever initiated the initial attachment to Arsenal; it had become very real and powerfully embedded in my friend's psyche, and obviously fulfilled some deeper purpose for him.

What I have also observed is that the intensity of these attachments become even more apparent when they are tested or when people are feeling unusually insecure for some reason. The obvious scenario where this takes place is when a nation is at war when the identification to the nation, or in the case of civil war, a particular cause, becomes extremely strong. The population becomes increasingly hostile and intolerant of any comment or action that they perceive as being unpatriotic. This is reflected in the attitude to genuinely peaceful people who stand by their ethical convictions and refuse to engage in violence by registering as conscientious objectors. In normal times humans with these qualities would be respected for their compassion to others but when the nation is at war the whole collective psyche of the community around them has suddenly changed and they frequently become objects of suspicion, derision and hostility.

I am absolutely humbled by reading stories about the courage of soldiers in the trenches in the First World War from whichever side they represented in this terrible conflict. When sent over the top in battle in the face of extreme danger, many of them actually genuinely expected to die. They were still however prepared to risk their lives for the attachment that they had formed to their concept of brotherhood, common cause or nation. It could be argued that this was the strict army discipline enforced though severe sanction, but it would take a considerable amount of time to overcome natural instincts for survival and many of these men were volunteers with only rudimental training. I have come to believe that the instinct to protect the object of powerful attachments is so instinctively ingrained in humanity that for some people it is more natural to even lay down their life than to betray this bond.

We are so accustomed to the attachments that people make that we do not take the time to stand outside of the human experience and look impartially at what is going on. From a rational perspective virtually none of these examples seems to make any sense, but we nearly all make these attachments and any threat to the object of our powerful links are likely to cause us significant distress. I am not remotely qualified to explain the reasons for HAB, and I am sure that this is familiar territory for any psychologists amongst my readers. I will therefore primarily make observations on how it manifests itself and some of what appear to be its main properties and consequences. I will also make suggestions as to how I believe HAB is severely restricting humanity's ability to evolve beyond some of its basest instincts.

ORB:- Come on Buzzard, help me here, how am I going to understand your peculiar species if you don't at least make some attempt to explain how HAB could have evolved?

Fair point, having stated how eminently unqualified I am in the sphere of psychology I can see no good reason why I can't take just a little time out to speculate on what may underlie such a strong manifestation of HAB in our species. I am sure there will be howls of indignation from those distinguished intellectuals who understand these things far better than I but after all, this book is nothing if not a deliberate provocation to my fellow humans.

Being a humble fan of Charles Darwin I will take the starting point that HAB must have had significant evolutionary advantages for the species and have enabled members of humanity in which HAB was particularly strong to compete more effectively than others in the population.

Certainly if we start with childbirth and parenting it is quite easy to highlight the potential advantages of HAB, particularly between a child and its mother. Human babies are born virtually helpless, partly because the sheer size of the human brain and its encasing skull provides a significant challenge to their mothers in giving birth. The clearance between the skull and parts of the female pelvis is very small as I am sure many mothers who have gone through this painful experience will be only too willing to testify. The human brain and skull still have a long way to develop before a child is even remotely capable of independent action. A strong emotional bond is therefore an obvious advantage if the new child is to be nurtured and supported through the vulnerable years of development though childhood and adolescence. When this bond of attachment is missing it can be highly traumatic for both mother and baby. It is certainly easy to imagine that in the earlier stages of human evolution such babies would have been highly vulnerable and far less likely to survive. This would certainly seem to support an evolutionary advantage to HAB between human mothers and their offspring.

We have already stated that HAB is also strongly manifest in attachments beyond the immediate bond to parents and other members in the immediate family group. Many examples have been offered of very strong emotional links where there is no obvious rational explanation as to why these should have been formed. It would appear that HAB within humans acts a bit like a bar of iron surrounded by magnets. Humans seem to have a natural hereditary propensity to make these attachments. If one attachment is broken they appear to be highly susceptible to making another should they come under its sphere of influence and this can sometimes be almost instantaneous. Why might this perhaps be an evolutionary advantage?

Humans seem to derive a significant competitive advantage when operating in groups and the larger the groups and the stronger the bonds of attachments, the more effective the advantage when competing for resources with other groups. This is quite evident in tribal cultures when the attachments to the tribal identity would seem to be a very significant advantage for survival. At time of high stress such as famine or warfare, the susceptibility of the members of the tribe to sacrifice themselves for the greater good of the tribal as a whole would certainly appear to offer evolutionary advantages. Early groupings where attachment behaviour was less prevalent may have found it very hard to compete with those where HAB was more pronounced, thereby giving a significant evolutionary advantage to tribes where HAB was most prevalent.

The ability for HAB to readjust and make new attachments can also be seen when tribal groupings band together to form some kind of larger grouping, perhaps a national identity, or a link through some other mechanism such as a common ideology. One of these other ideologies is something that we refer to as a religion and when religion is combined with nationalism HAB can become immensely powerful. All normal checks and balances on behaviour can virtually disappear when nationalistic and religious fervour is stimulated in those belonging to a collective group.

The successful tribal and national leaders throughout the history of my species have instinctively understood the advantage to be had through making an alignment with a prevailing religion. Religions ideas can be seen to spread somewhat in the manner of a viral contagion when linked to successful societal groupings. This can be seen by looking at our planet and where the different religions are particularly prevalent. The spread of Christianity is very much linked to the Roman Empire which adopted it around 312 CE (common dating era) through the Emperor Constantine. This was subsequently further spread by Christian influenced European Empires throughout other parts of the world such as North and South America, Australasia and many parts of Africa.

Islam very successfully spread through groupings such as the Umayyads, Abbasids, Fatimids, Ghaznavids, Seljuqs, Safavids, Mughals, and the Ottoman Empire to cover most of North Africa, what we now call the middle East and into Asia and the Indian subcontinent. At its height it even successfully spread to mainland Spain through numerous military successes. The Hindu religion equally predominates in India where it evolved as an intrinsic part of the established culture of tribal groupings within that geographical sphere.

It is only in relatively recent human history that different religious and ethnic groups have been less fixed by geography and are now increasingly living together within countries. This is creating some significant tensions within some of these societies. There is increasing evidence of conflicts between the HAB manifest towards the national institutions and cultures and the HAB towards the religious cultures and directives. These two objects of attachment are for some in modern societies becomingly increasingly conflicting. For most of the history of humanity these have been largely intertwined and complementary. This is by no means coincidental as it has been deliberately engineered through the active collusion of the political and religious powerbrokers. The objective of this collusion has been to powerfully influence and indeed, deliberately manipulate the mass of humans under their sphere of control using the embedded properties of HAB.

Some in society believe that it is necessary to mitigate the more extreme aspects of certain religions to be compatible with the culture, norms and values prevalent in the established society. In stark contrast others, where their HAB to religious ideology is stronger than their cultural attachments, would change the established norms and values of their adopted society to conform to religious values. This is manifest in my own country where increasingly, some followers of the Islamic faith wish to exercise the constraints of religious or Sharia law within their local communities, even creating Sharia courts with the complicity of the UK Government. This is causing increasing disquiet in the population who strongly disagree with the religious ideology underpinning Sharia law and those who promote these values, and see it as a threat to more established and prevalent cultures. Both of these approaches create significant tensions in society as HAB to the culture, norms and values of both religion and established society can be extremely strong. Should this tension escalate it can be expected that the reaction of the different groupings, should they perceive the object of their HAB to be under threat, will become increasingly confrontational. This should be of some serious concern to all.

Chapter 2 – An exploration of the relationship between human attachment behaviour (HAB) and religion

ORB:- I don't really understand this thing you call religion. What makes it so different to any other tribal or national customs and why are the leaders of successful human groups so keen to spread and support it?

A very good and fundamental question my rational friend, I am going to focus considerable attention on the human religions. This is for two key reasons:

1. Religions represent some of the very strangest and yet most powerful of all human attachments and are therefore highly illustrative of HAB's properties.

2. Religions continue to affect the behaviour of a large percentage of the human population and in many cases can be a source of considerable anxiety, strife, intolerance and hostility between groups of people that segregate along religious lines.

In the latter part of the book I will look at humanity's dire addiction to uncontrolled greed which in many ways parallels a form of religion and certainly gets well and truly mixed up with them.

Humans intrinsically believe that they know what a religion is and even protect the right to believe in the staggering variety of different religions in their laws. In fact the single term religion is used extensively for a whole plethora of disparate beliefs belonging to humans, many of which are entirely different in nature. This can cause considerable confusion and difficulties, particularly when secular authorities try to apply consistent policies to groups with very different ideas and objectives. The one element that most religions do require is some element of faith, a form of HAB that supersedes rational examination. It is this element of faith that separates religions from theories produced through scientific enquiry which relies upon evidence. In the scientific world, theories based upon evidence are put up to be actively challenged through observation or further experimentation in the search to get nearer to the truth of things. Often the objects of faith for these religions are a perceived higher order of beings that are supposed to influence the life of humans. These are referred to as Gods for the religions that maintain that there are a number of these beings or deities that assert their wills upon our species or simply as God when a religion maintains that there is just the one.

This form of HAB referred to as faith, linked to God or the Gods is also sometimes referred to as belief or devotion, and those belonging to religions may therefore be referred to as devotees, the faithful or believers. Most of the hierarchy that run these various religions usually demand unquestioning faith from the "faithful". This is the complete opposite of the scientific approach and in most religions any attempt to question the assumptions or sacred texts is usually met with considerable hostility. The ones that welcome challenges and questioning of their ideas are very different in character to the ones that insist on unquestioning faith and I shall focus much more on this in due course.

Unquestioning faith is one of the most malevolent and damaging aspects of behaviour that is demanded by faith based religions and their leaders as it absolves the faithful from the obligation to exercise rational scrutiny of their actions. This puts a frightening amount of power in the hands of those appointed by the religious authorities to guide the faithful. History has shown that the power possessing individuals within religions and their followers are quite prepared to encourage the faithful to extinguish the lives of fellow humans who do not share their views or who they perceive to be a threat. I intend to delve into this and other malevolent properties of religions and their devotees in much greater detail later in our conversation. This antagonism towards fellow humans with differing beliefs is usually justified as being carried out in the name of whichever God supposedly oversees the actions of the faithful. The appointed officers of these religions claim to be able to interpret the intentions of their God or Gods (which universally cannot be conversed with in any rational sense of the word) and as a result they claim the right to be able to dictate the actions required of the faithful through what they refer to as divine authority. The real reason that these instructions are issued is to meet the various human needs of these appointed officers and their personal egos and ambitions.

ORB:- *"I am finding this a bit difficult to understand. Are you saying that humanity sometimes turns upon itself and humans are prepared to even destroy each other's lives on the basis of myths and superstitions supported by no objective evidence?"*

I am afraid so, I think you are starting to get an understanding as to just how HAB can have such a significant and often detrimental effect on the lives of us humans. Back to your earlier question of how do we define a religion. For the purposes of this book I shall define a religion as an identifiable doctrine with its own set of beliefs, values and cultural associations that are not dependent upon any rational evidence to underpin its particular worldview. As stated, usually a religion will have a "religious" text or texts that define its particular perspective on the world and an associated set of specific rules and customs and authority figures that the believers have to follow. Above all these religions each claim to exclusively reveal the ultimate word of the God or Gods through their religious texts, which they will claim can only truly be interpreted by these empowered authority figures. This places considerable power into the hands of the officers of these religions over the rest of the humans in their societies.

There are however other doctrines that are commonly defined using the term religion and which actually require those that follow them to independently seek after the truth of things and to be enquiring at all times. The purpose of these doctrines is for the follower to obtain a degree of what is called enlightenment and escape the more malevolent properties of HAB. One of these is called by humans Buddhism, but there are others existing both now and in the history of the human species. I intend to separate these from the mainstream of religions which rely on unquestioning faith. I shall call these doctrines or teachings "wisdom traditions" as opposed to religions although most of my fellow humans would not readily understand the distinction.

Wisdom traditions are unfortunately not always led or influenced by the wise as they also rely on a number of authority figures and "teachers" who are supposed to guide the followers towards a higher level of understanding. The difficulty for devotees of these wisdom traditions is to find a teacher who has actually attained a higher level of reasoning rather than a nefarious individual who has adopted this role to meet the needs of their own ego and ambition. You can however at least applaud the ambition and goals of wisdom traditions despite these difficulties. The other advantage of wisdom traditions is that there are many common aspects amongst them regarding the higher potential for human development and understanding that the seeker can draw upon on their own personal journey. We shall explore these a bit later on.

In order to make it clear to the reader which of these types of religion I am referring to I shall refer to "God faiths" for those religions requiring unquestioning devotion and "wisdom traditions" for those actively encouraging followers to seek an enhanced understanding of themselves.

ORB; "I am still struggling to understand these God beings who are supposed to exist. What are they and what evidence do you humans have for their existence that incites such intense passion?"

I was expecting, and somewhat dreading this question. Belief in God or Gods is one of the very strangest aspects of HAB. Whole civilisations have risen and fallen over differences of opinion on who or what God is. It is one of the very strongest attachments that humans make and in many cases humans are entirely prepared to even sacrifice their lives (and with even more enthusiasm, the lives of others) in what they believe is service to their God.

The one thing that is almost entirely certain is that humans do not know the nature of their God or Gods but the faithful will try to draw conclusions from their religious texts. The officers of these religions, which in the religion called Christianity, are called priests, bishops, archbishops, cardinals or popes, depending on where they sit in the established hierarchy, assert that they are uniquely empowered to interpret what they like to call the "will of God". These officers hold great influence over many within the community. Those devotees following whichever religion predominates within their culture and community believe that these officers have a genuine insight into the nature of their God and in particular the interpretation of whichever text is supposed to reflect their God's will.

There are many different religions in the world, some of these are larger than others but even the largest are split into many squabbling factions. Each of these will firmly argue that their particular interpretation is the absolute truth, which by definition implies that all of the others have been misled and are actually ignorant of the truth.

ORB:- but this doesn't make sense. Surely from what you have told me it is statistically improbable that any of these religious factions knows the truth and therefore it is highly unlikely that any single one of them is more correct that any other?

My dear friend, you will rapidly become extremely unpopular with the faithful if you start using rational logic such as statistical probability. Once fully indoctrinated into their particular faith, firmly establishing the malevolent properties of their HAB, it would never occur to the faithful that they might have been horribly misguided. For most of human history, the established secular and religious powers would most certainly have extinguished your life for making such an assertion.

I have personally struggled with this question for most of my life. Like most young children I was initially indoctrinated through the education process in the particular faith that was customary for my country and community at the time. The God faith into which I was indoctrinated was called Christianity and the particular faction of this God faith was known as the Church of England. This faction uses a book, in common with other Christian factions, called "the Bible" as its principle religious text which was supposed to reflect the truth and the unquestionable "word of God".

This is one of the more disturbing aspects of HAB in that the parents and schools associated with a particular religion almost always see it as a primary duty to try to establish a strong attachment to their religion in their children's psyches from a very young age. This perpetuates the myths and customs of the society which we have already discussed has in the past had significant evolutionary advantages. To those humans with an inclination towards rational objectivity like ORB's, this is an anathema as it creates great barriers for every human to overcome should they ever decide to actively seek out the truth of things. It is much easier and often much more comforting to conform with the established order of a culture or society with its rules and customs than to stand apart and, feeling at best isolated and alone, and at worst subject to active hostility that could endanger life itself.

The start of my personal escape from the attachment of religion in my HAB, established by school and related institutions, began when I had reached the age of five years. I can still vividly remember my teacher at the time saying that some archaeologists had found some old timbers on a mountain in a place called Sinai and this proved that one of the stories in the Christian religious book called the Bible must be true. The implication was that if one story was true then it must all be true and hence there was unequivocal evidence for the existence of God as portrayed in this Bible. This particular story was called Noah's Ark. It asserts that God had got very angry that humans were not behaving well and worshiping him enough and that he (yes strangely the Christians have sexed their God as male) would therefore drown every man woman and child on the planet except Noah and his family. Not a particularly capable God as it states in the Bible that God created these same humans and he obviously came up with a pretty flawed design. Believe it or not Christians call their God compassionate, but more on this later.

This story leaves the problem that all the other beings on the planet would have been drowned too and, as we know, there are many millions of different beings still here. The story got over this troublesome fact by saying that dear old Noah built a big boat called "the Ark" in which he took one breeding pair of every species on the planet so that that the planet could be repopulated after God had committed his mass slaughter of most of the Earth's beings in his fit of vengeful petulance.

Now I have to confess that at the age of five my rational capacity for thought was still in an early stage of development so I rushed back to my parents to share the good news that God actually existed! My father had always been a follower of scientific thinking and not particularly prone to adopting a "God faith" but, to be fair, he never tried to stop my propensity as a human for my HAB to attach me to such a thing. He did however sit down and talk this through. We talked about the number of animals in the world, how far apart they were and just how big Noah's boat would have to be to accommodate all these beings. He then posed the question, is it more probable that the story of Noah's Ark was true or was it more probable that it was just a good but mythical tale and perhaps all the people and beings on the planet didn't drown after all? Even to my poorly developed reason it was so completely unlikely that the tale was true that I became firmly convinced that it was just an entertaining myth.

This did however pose a slightly more difficult question. If this tale was a myth then what about the rest of this book called the Bible and more importantly what about God himself? I decided that I would assume that the God of my particular "God faith" was also a myth. This was quite straightforward as I had already been told by the officers of my religion that everyone else's God was already a myth and it was therefore just one more to add to a growing list. I decided that I would only believe in the existence of God if I actually found any reasonable evidence to support such an assertion. I am still waiting for some even vaguely tentative evidence to even suggest the existence of such a being as God nearly fifty years later (ok, you have got me, I am no longer in my first flush of youth!).

The other outcome that has caused me some considerable difficulty and consternation since this time is that I stopped believing that teachers, so called experts, and those in authority actually knew the truth of things. This has led me to question everything I hear and give it my own test of rationality or probability. If what I am being told fails this personal test then I will be inclined to reject what is being proposed and treat the associated expert with considerable caution with regard to their future assertions. If what I am being told seems persuasive then I will add this piece of information to my meagre database and view the world from a slightly different perspective than I did before. I would of course encourage every reader to treat every view that I express in this book to a similar personal test because, as I have already attested, nothing I write as a human being can ever be considered to be true. It is just my latest personal perspective on the way I see the world based on the information I have managed to accumulate at the time of writing.

I often fret that I have been burdened with a mind that seems so demanding and frequently wish it would just shut up or, "chill out." I have also at times become somewhat unpopular as I can be prone to challenge authority figures who I do not believe have made a rational case to support their decisions or actions. This has not been generally met with appreciation by many of these figures. Teachers, professors, members of management boards, politicians, senior economists and in particular many officers of religions believe that their status and "position" in the hierarchy of society endow their particular perspective with a greater authority than that of others. Anyone who challenges this assumed authority is often given very short shrift. It is also in the human nature of many of my species that when they feel that they have been affronted they exercise a manifestation which is called revenge; in that they may actively seek to damage the prospects of those who they perceived have given them a personal slight.

I have a wonderfully patient soul mate with whom I have been uniquely privileged to travel in partnership through life's journey who has patiently suffered as a result of this particularly difficult aspect of my personality. Sometimes these disagreements with authority figures are associated with something within that I call my "ethics" for want of a better description. I shall discuss ethics at greater length when examining some of the positive aspects of "wisdom traditions" later in this book. These disagreements have at times ended up with the Buzzard leaving what could be considered lucrative employment, much to the financial disadvantage of not only the Buzzard but also his long suffering partner!

ORB:- I believe you are wandering off the path of our discussion here Buzzard. Getting back to the theme of Gods, it seems rather unlikely that you will be able tell me much about these entities as perceived in the minds of the faithful, if you don't actually believe that they exist!

Fear not; fortunately we can draw on the sacred texts of these "God faiths" to try to understand what God is supposed to be like. The bigger question is why so many humans can believe that their particular "God faith" is true when the actual evidence for such a belief can be brought under question by the poorly developed rationality of a young human child.

ORB:- So how many humans actually follow a God faith?

This is actually a very difficult question to answer. There are "God faiths" such as Christianity, Judaism, and Islam which commonly follow either "the Bible" or related texts. There are other religions such as Hinduism which on the surface look like "God faiths" and which are considered as such by many of their believers but which on deeper examination show underpinning evidence that they are actually a wisdom tradition. This is another worrying aspect of HAB in that many who have made an attachment to a religion have never actually tried to understand their own religious texts. They have made an attachment to some picture in their psyche that represents what their particular religion means to them. I have talked to many Christians who have never read the Bible and whose picture of their God, when discussed, bears absolutely no relationship with the nature of God as portrayed in the Bible at all. In addition to the fact that many followers of God faiths don't actually understand the nature of what they are following, their numbers are often estimated on the basis of the geographic location or cultural heritage of the populations associated with them. Any estimates are therefore most probably greatly exaggerated.

If we were to take Hinduism as a "God faith" (I will later assert that I don't actually believe it is) then we can try to estimate the main "God faith" religions of Christianity, Islam and Hinduism. There are many more minor "God faiths" or obscure splinter groups of the main ones. I shall shamelessly steal the following figures from the dear people's encyclopaedia Wikipedia (http://en.wikipedia.org/wiki/List_of_religious_populations) which I know will cause all academics to rage with indignation but hey, this is a book about HAB not statistics! At the time of writing, dear Wiki estimates that there are between 1.9 and 2.1 billion Christians, roughly 1.7 billion Muslims (followers of Islam) and about 1 billion Hindus. This amounts to between 63% and 71% of the population of humans on Earth. My instincts are that this is an exaggeration as in many parts of the world it is virtually unacceptable within a culture to admit that you don't follow a "God faith" so I would hazard a guess that genuine believers comprise roughly 50 - 60% of the Earth's population. This is still an extraordinary statistical illustration of the power of the HAB to overcome objective reasoning. It is also important to understand that those humans whose HAB is not attached to a God faith will in all probability have created an attachment to something else which may be similarly improbable.

ORB:- Let me get this clear, what you are saying is over half the total population of humans have created a relationship with a God or Gods for which there is no objective of their existence? You are also implying that they argue or even kill each other over which mythical being is true or who has the best interpretation of a particular God's nature?

I know that this is very hard to explain and what you must find even more surprising is that humanity sees nothing strange in this and that many humans believing in "God faiths" also consider themselves to be fully rational beings. As previously stated "God faiths" are even allowed to run schools so that the human attachment behaviour (HAB) of different cultures to the approved "God faith" can be firmly established in the vulnerable minds of human children. I have always found this a particularly interesting aspect of our so called "civilised" societies. We know from very elementary mathematical statistics that in all probability any particular "God Faith" is statistically unlikely to be true, and therefore probably none of them are. All the different splinter groups of these various faiths and their associated religious authorities are therefore actively misleading their fellow humans although through the power of their own HAB to their God faith they will genuinely not believe this to be true. Society however has endowed "God Faiths" as bastions of morality (I shall also deal with the word morality when I also talk about ethics a bit later). So despite the obvious statistical irrationality of such an approach, many humans and their political leaders see the indoctrination of children into a God faith as a very positive thing. We therefore have our leaders knowingly and actively encouraging our children to be systematically programmed with various myths. Shouldn't we rather be encouraging them to follow a path of reasoned observation and being taught to draw their own conclusions based on the strength of the evidence presented to them? We humans are systematically handicapping the reason of each succeeding generation at the most vulnerable time in its development.

ORB:- Now I am really confused, why on earth would any species want to programme its young people with contradictory myths if it wishes to evolve? Surely the future of your species is in the hands of the young and therefore their education and the development of their reasoning abilities should be treated with the utmost care?

Ah ha, you have now struck at the heart of things and the fundamental question that overshadows this whole written enterprise! Does humanity want to evolve or is it in fact in the interests of the power possessing individuals within our species to ensure that humanity doesn't evolve? Certainly an evolved species would never put up with the staggering inequality and exploitation manifest in humanity today. It could therefore be argued that it is very much in the perceived interests of those who most benefit (benefit in financial terms and in attracting accolade for their needy egos rather than as a human being) to ensure that the human species does anything but evolve. I will however argue later in this enterprise of mine that most of these power possessing humans actually cause themselves considerable harm as well as causing great harm and suffering to their fellow humans through their actions.

Chapter 3 - Speculation on the properties of the human psyche

ORB:- ego?

Now you have really got me, I was rather hoping that we could avoid the topic of ego but I now think that this will be unavoidable and perhaps we should just take a short detour from the theme of Gods to explore this word. I am sure that my dear fellow humans with an interest in psychiatry or other disciplines that study the human mind will recoil in horror at my attempts to explain the ego and the impact that it can have upon us. I think the only reasonable outcome from my attempt at this task will be for me to create a model and understanding of what I mean by this term when I use it in the context of the pages of this book.

Ego is a word that is largely associated with the work of a particularly intelligent and analytical man by the name of Sigmund Freud. I personally find Freud helpful and I shall therefore draw on some of his ideas to explain what I mean by ego and why I think it is so important when looking at the peculiarities of my strange species. Looking at HAB we have already made reference to powerful instinctive and emotional drivers that seem to have such a powerful influence upon the rationality of human actions. These drivers are largely unconscious, humans don't consciously decide to have an emotional reaction to something, get sexually attracted or to have a fear inducing phobias about spiders, snakes etc. These instincts and emotions manifest themselves from the unconscious whilst the conscious mind then takes note and wrestles, not always with a great deal of success, to mitigate the influence of these subconscious drivers of behaviour.

Freud created a model of the human mind, or psyche to try to explain the dynamics of what he observed in people during analysis of his fellow humans, particularly in cases where these dynamics were causing significant imbalances or distress. Freud called the unconscious, instinctive element of the human psyche the id and the conscious element the ego which he described as an evolved adaptation of part of the id enabling the human mind to perceive the external environment and make appropriate decisions for survival. Freud's model has been frequently challenged by fellow humans who have an interest in the workings of the human psyche known as psychologists. I personally have found a resonance in his ideas with my own self observation and observation of others within my peculiar species. I also find a beautiful simplicity in his model which makes an extremely useful framework for looking at the properties of HAB and where these might originate.

One aspect of Freud's model was that the unconscious id systematically makes emotional attachments (or investments), to objects, people or ideas. Freud called such an emotional attachment a cathexis. As part of the ego's relationship with the id it can identify or internalise these emotional attachments and either give in to their influence or try to resist or suppress them. This is particularly important to the efficient functioning and survival of a human as it is the ego's job to evaluate the urges induced through a cathexis in the context of the external environment in which the human is embedded. The ego may decide that giving in to an impulse arising from a cathexis is not in the human's best interests and may threaten its ability to compete or even survive. Resisting a cathexis is however not without consequence for the ego as such a repression causes tension within the human psyche. The more powerful the attachment or the weaker the ego, the less likely it is that these attachments can be successfully repressed or the greater the psychological stress arising from such a repression.

The ability of the human's unconscious mind to make these emotional attachments to objects of affection or ideas will be revisited later as this gives an interesting clue as to why some amongst my species appear to have an unquenchable desire to acquire objects and money (capital). This can have catastrophic impacts on the rest of the species as resources are horded to the severe detriment of society. This is so endemic in the human species that it is barely questioned and this slavery to the greed arising from this cathexic desire is actually seen as a positive trait rather than a curse. This is why in countries such as the United States of America, those particularly addicted to hoarding to satisfy their cathexic desires actually seem quite content to see fellow humans in their society die from preventable health issues or malnutrition as a consequence. The right to be a slave to the attachment behaviour of their id, unconstrained by their needy underdeveloped ego, is seen as more important than poverty, ill health and ultimately the deaths of fellow humans.

Another aspect of the ego according to this model is that it strives to be "loved", either by the id (its own unconscious self), or in substitute by these objects of emotional attachment. This makes particular sense when we looked earlier at some examples of emotional attachment and the genuine distress caused when the object of this attachment was harmed. It would appear that, as the ego becomes more developed, it becomes less dependent on the need for internal or external love and attention for its own sense of security and independence. This development is by no means assured and often requires constant striving by the individual human to overcome the emotional and instinctive tempests that can rage within the unconscious id. I believe it is this battle for self-development and rational understanding within the ego, overcoming the powerful emotional and instinctive forces within id, which underpins many of the key principles to be found in the teachings of the aforementioned wisdom traditions. I shall focus a lot more on this later on.

There is another element to Freud's model that is particularly helpful to our understanding of what initially appear to be unexplainable attachments to religious ideas and authority figures. This additional element in the model is called the super-ego or ego-ideal and is argued to originate with the early exposure of the newly born human to a powerful authority figure. The first powerful emotional attachment is made between the new-born and its mother but it rapidly becomes aware of another being also competing for the affections of the mother in the form of the father figure (or any other significant figure competing for the mother's attentions). This figure becomes initially an object of hostility, indeed Freud would assert that the child would instinctively like to eliminate this object of emotional competition if it had the strength and the means. Freud called this the Oedipus complex after a figure from historical mythology who mistakenly kills his father and ends up marrying his mother. The human child deals with the hostility to this powerful competitor for the mother's affection by creating an internal identification with them through the development of part of the id. This part of the unconscious id that creates its own particular properties is called the super-ego or as I shall continue to refer to it the ego-ideal. The ego-ideal is very much grounded into the instinctive nature of the id and acts to constrain the independence of the ego on behalf of the id, aiming to place a limitation on the ego's choices. Conflict by the conscious ego against the emotions and behavioural constraints demanded from the ego-ideal manifest themselves in a number of uncomfortable emotions such as guilt, embarrassment or even self-contempt and resulting depression. The ego-ideal is in effect holding up an "idealised" model of the desires of the unconscious id and holds the ego to account when it falls short of this idealised concept.

Figures of authority or strong beliefs and ideas within society also create identification within the developing ego-ideal which can also then act as a constraint on the ego. This is particularly powerful when the ego is still weak and underdeveloped as in young children and this is one reason why religions and established societies are so keen to get access to the young at the earliest possible opportunity. The authority of the religion embedded through an identification within the ego-ideal and acts as a severe constraint on the development of independent thought based on logical reasoning within the ego. Any attempt by the ego to draw away from the influence of these religious ideals is then met with terrible feelings of guilt and isolation within the ego, as the ego-ideal rages against it. It is a battle that the ego can win but it is often a very significant event or betrayal that is required to break the attachment to such a powerfully reinforced identification. Nationalism is another trait that is equally susceptible to this process, loyalty to a sense of belonging in the concept of a nation creating a powerful identification in the ego-ideal.

As the ego-ideal is very firmly grounded in the instinctive and emotional drivers in the human id, and a sense of threat or insecurity perceived by the ego through the senses can rapidly enhance the power of these identifications in the ego-ideal. This increase in the power of the unconscious impulses, manifest through the ego-ideal can sometimes overcome any attempt within the ego to deploy rational and constraining logic. Any group of humans that are linked by a common identification within their ego-ideals such as a religion, nationalism or political dogma can collectively react to threats to the object of their collective identification in ways that would normally seem completely irrational. All ruling politicians exploit this trait to a greater or lesser extent when trying to influence populations for their own ends. The political models that give leaders more influence and power, such as dictatorships, can enable manipulation of these instinctive drivers to a great degree.

I believe it is such a policy of deliberate manipulation of nationalistic drivers that enabled a particularly malign human from history called Adolf Hitler to collectively influence the psyche of many of the people in a country called Germany with devastating results. In particular he persuasively convinced many German nationals that certain ethnic and political groups with distinctive cultures within the country were a threat to national wellbeing. This deliberate manipulation of the collective cathexis of the German people to the concept of nationhood, combined with a deliberately created threat to this object of attachment through the properties of HAB, incited otherwise rational beings to commit very irrational and appalling collective retribution on these groups. This deliberate emotional manipulation of mass populations by politicians and other influential beings within societies such as religious leaders has continued throughout human history and is still very prevalent today.

It is a specific attribute of the relationship between the ego and the ego-ideal that, by aligning itself to the unconscious yet powerful demands of the ego-ideal, the ego eliminates much of the source of guilt and tension. This surrender to powerful emotional drivers can create a sense of virtual euphoria, particularly when this experience is shared with a large mass of fellow beings with a common attachment. Going to my previous example, any look at the historical footage of rallies in the German city of Nuremburg can see this extraordinary powerful process utterly manifest. The more powerful and fearful the threats and sanctions imposed by the regime, the stronger the emotional attachment that is manifest through the stimulation of the survival instinct in the id. This powerful impulse is executed by the ego-ideal as a constraint on any resistance from the rational ego.

It is through this rather complex, but extraordinarily powerful mechanism that HAB becomes firmly established with institutions and ideas. It is absolutely no accident that for much of the recorded history of my strange species, political leaders and tyrants have always strived to associate themselves with the prevailing religion and equally the religious hierarchy have sought to associate themselves with the prevailing secular authorities. This alignment of strong identifications within the ego-ideal makes the population even more compliant to the perceived authority of power possessing individuals within these institutions.

ORB:- I am not so sure I am glad I asked about my question about the ego after all that! Could you perhaps summarise this rather lengthy explanation for me?

I shall attempt to do so. The human brain or psyche in my Freudian based model is split into three parts, the ego, the id and ego-ideal. The ego is an evolved part of the human psyche that adapts to the perception of the outside world obtained through the senses. It uses the information and stimuli received through the senses to attempt to consciously safeguard the wellbeing of the human in the context of the environment and potential threats outside the human body. The id contains powerful unconscious emotional and instinctive drivers that significantly influence the id providing the internal emotional context to the actions of the ego. In extreme cases the emotional and instinctive impulses are so powerful they can completely override resistance in the ego resulting in the most severe cases in being an actual instigator of the human's death. The id's first powerful emotional attachments to outside objects first manifest in the very powerful attachment to the mother. Freud calls such an attachment a cathexis and is in the context of this book a powerful example of HAB.

The id is initially at birth constrained by powerful outside figures of authority who compete for affection from the mother and which the id initially rages against but which the helpless baby is too weak to do anything about. The psyche overcomes this by creating identifications with such figures in a further development of the id that Freud calls the ego-ideal. This constrains the ego at the behest of the id as an internalised and legitimised representative of these external authority figures, embedded within the psyche or brain. Early programming of the ego-ideal whilst the ego is immature and weak enables these external figures and associated ideas to hold powerful sway over the future behaviour and compliance of the developing human by constraining the ego. It is this deliberate and systematic programming of the young through the structured organisations associated with them that has enabled religions to replicate themselves in every generation. It is however true that in the more liberal of the world's societies the grip of religions are slowly starting to falter as they become subject to a growing scrutiny of their more blatant contradictions and the further revelations of scientific enquiry. This is particularly true of "God faiths".

It might help understanding to introduce a quick metaphor here to help explain the relationships as I have perceived them between the id, the ego-ideal and the ego. In the human world there are various murky but extremely powerful criminal organisations that operate in the shadows and dark corners of society. One of the most famous was (is still) called the Mafia and the Mafia would have amongst its ranks certain individuals called enforcers who would use threats and intimidation to persuade other humans within society to comply with the Mafia's will. If you were for instance to place yourself in the position of a businessman just starting up in an area with a Mafia influence, you could expect to get a knock on the door from the Mafia's local enforcer. This will be your only contact with the Mafia over which you have no control or influence and many would deny even its existence. The enforcer would try to intimidate you and dictate which suppliers and carriers you were allowed to use and take a cut of any profits. You have no control over which suppliers the Mafia has attached itself to, no matter how inefficient and sloppy their service might be, they can do pretty much as they choose. Your rational mind will tell you that there are better suppliers and carriers that you could use that would make your business more profitable but there is a cost to standing up to the enforcer. Should you choose to defy the enforcer there are consequences, you might find your windows broken, valued customers may be warned against using your business, you may be subjected to violence or even death. There is potential help to be had, you can ask the police and the authorities to get involved but this requires caution as they may have also been infiltrated by the Mafia so you must choose your help with care. This leaves you with a stark choice, run your business accepting that the Mafia is a necessary evil for a quiet life, or exert your independence and stand up to the enforcer knowing that there will be a hard price to pay for the benefits and freedom that come with business independence.

Let's now put this scenario into the id, the ego-ideal and the ego. The id is the Mafia over which you have no control and is hidden in the shadows of your psyche yet exerts a powerful influence in all that goes on. The ego-ideal is the enforcer, part of the id but the part that seeks to exert the id's influence on the ego. The ego is the poor businessperson who at birth starts their business on the id's (the psyche's Mafia) turf. The ego has no influence over what attachments the id makes no matter how irrational these may be, but if it defies them it can expect to have a visit from the ego-ideal, the id's enforcer. Any attempts to stand up to the demands made by the ego-ideal may have serious consequences. In the psyche the retribution meted out is not broken windows or physical violence but can be equally distressing. The symptoms of this conflict are anxiety, stress, depression, anger and in the most severe situations self-loathing that may lead to self-harm or suicide. There are people who you can call on to help in these battles and their advice can be found in both established health professionals and also within the wisdom traditions where people have fought these battles over the ages and you can learn from their experience. A word of warning however, not all the advice that will be offered will be wise so you must use your cognitive capabilities to weed out that which resonates and you perceive to be true. Otherwise you may find that the givers of advice are actually in collusion with the objects of attachments already made within your id and you may become even more enslaved. Like the businessman, the ego's (the businessperson) fight against the demands of the id (Mafia), relayed through the ego-ideal (the Mafia's enforcer), is not an easy one. The ego may decide to succumb to the id's emotional pressure for an easier life, but resisting these unconscious demands and subjecting them to rational scrutiny is a human's only route to true liberation and having genuine control over your own psyche and your resulting actions.

Has this helped?

ORB:- What a bizarre set up, it is amazing that your species hasn't managed to follow other species like the dinosaurs on the path to extinction yet! No wonder you behave so irrationally. It must be extraordinarily difficult to be a human having the conscious element of your brains constantly bombarded and overwhelmed from all sides by powerful instinctive impulses and strange emotional attachments over which you would appear to have very little control.

Do I detect a very welcome note of sympathy over our plight? If only we humans would be so kind and understanding of ourselves. Unfortunately most of our institutions and particularly some of our most influential religions simply seem to want to punish us for the unfortunate construction of our human psyche. It is certainly not in the interest of God faith based religions for the human ego to start making independent rational judgements after so much effort has been spent creating strong attachments in the id. This is an important lesson for us as a species if we truly decide we wish to evolve, it is really about time we humans cut ourselves a little slack and allow ourselves a little more understanding, compassion and kindness. We are indeed highly vulnerable to manipulation both from within our psyches and from exterior manipulation by those who instinctively understand our natures. The power possessing individuals amongst us strongly desire humanity to continue to exist with a sense of embedded guilt over our so called sins and weaknesses. They shamelessly manipulate us through the vulnerabilities of our psyches for their own purposes. This has been a story repeated throughout our recorded history and will continue unless we collectively decide to acknowledge our true nature and the constraints it brings. It is only by truly accepting and recognising our susceptibilities as a species that we have any possibility to further evolve.

Chapter 4 – Wisdom traditions and God Faiths

ORB:- You have often used the term "wisdom traditions" as opposed to "God faiths. What do you consider the word wisdom to actually mean in the context of religion and its influence over the psyches of humans?

This is again a somewhat difficult question to answer but I shall have a stab at it, at least from my own perspective, in full recognition that many others from my species will most probably profoundly disagree with me (as is their inalienable right). I think the most important thing is to establish what I mean when using the words information and essence. I believe this is one of the most important things to reflect upon when evaluating the actions of humans. By my definition, wisdom is the combination of information set in the context of a developed essence. This essence is formed through a considerable personal commitment to the development of a true understanding of the nature of ourselves and the properties of our human psyches.

We humans live at a time of unparalleled access to information, an information age available at the click of a button through a large range of different mediums, the most comprehensive of which being the Internet. We also live in an age where our scientists are delving into the very building blocks of life and the elements and laws that govern the very fabric of our universe. I would assert however that despite this expediential increase in information, humanity has not been blessed with an equivalent increase in essence and hence rarely seems to act wisely.

Let me give a very contemporary example to illustrate the point that I am trying to make. As I write this at the start of the year 2012 CE the traditional powerful economies in Europe, the USA and Japan have been suffering from a dramatic economic collapse. Up until 2008 there was a collective blindness to the vast amounts of speculation going on in our financial services industries. Humanity appeared to be completely ignorant of the harsh reality that financial speculation in global markets was being used as a deliberate vehicle by a small but powerful minority addicted to growing their individual capital hoards at the expense of others. The unsuspecting mass of my species living in these countries were led to believe that this speculation would lead to enhanced prosperity for all while in fact it was a straightforward mechanism for the exploitation of the few at the expense of the many. Any analysis of average earnings, particularly in countries such as the USA and the UK, particularly enthusiastic advocates of the worth of capital exploitation, would have seen that this hadn't in fact been true for many years but was just convenient propaganda for those profiting from this situation.

Devising the extraordinary financial products such as "collateralized debt obligations" which magically turned junk "sub-prime" mortgage investments into AAA rated financial assets took a great deal of knowledge of the frailties in the design of capital markets. In fact these and other similar mechanisms were so clever that none of the regulators of the market really had any idea what was going on until the whole financial artifice collapsed. Exploiting this knowledge was done by people without any evidence of compassion or responsibility towards their fellow humans. These people knew that the whole financial edifice was rotten in the core but used the intervening period between their creation and collapse to extract vast wealth from these national economies for their own purposes.

These actions and many more like them have actively damaged the societies in which these same humans exist and into which they bring new offspring of their own. We have already discussed that this HAB to the continuous growth of personal capital is fuelled from attachments in the unconscious that are imposed upon the needy egos of these people through the ego-ideal. Rather than bringing these individuals any contentment in their lives, such action merely creates further cravings in their unconscious.

If the bankers and traders within our financial institutions had consciously worked on the development of their egos to be free of the instinctive self-focused impulses, very different decisions would have been made. In particular, free from the all-consuming appetite to feed their material cravings, their knowledge could have been used to invest in projects and industries that would actively increase collective wellbeing in society and benefit rather than harm their fellow human beings. Instead the inner contempt manifest through their punished and needy egos was externally focused on exploiting the vulnerable in their communities. This lack of compassion and care for the consequences of their actions clearly demonstrate what I would call a lack of essence in both the individuals concerned and the institutions that act as an amplification of their collective psyches.

What we have is a situation where vast amounts of information and intelligence is used extremely unwisely by those severely lacking in essence, to the great detriment of the societies they live in and their fellow humans exposed to these actions.

The big lesson for my species from this is that information and intelligence without essence frequently leads to very unwise actions that can cause incalculable harm. Wise action therefore requires a balance in both acquired knowledge and acquired essence and this is by no means an easy aspiration to achieve. Just look at how the history of my poor species is full of incidents where we have literally slaughtered each other by the millions to feed the irrational appetites of a few desperately unloved and needy egos amongst those in positions of power and influence.

ORB:- if I am starting to understand you correctly, you seem to be correlating essence with the development and maturity of the ego within human beings.

Got it in a nutshell! I am proposing that when a human child is born, nearly all its actions are dominated by instinctive emotions and drivers within its unconscious id. The release into an external world promotes the development of the ego and this has the capacity to grow in strength and influence as the human grows and ages. It also similarly promotes the development of the ego-ideal which acts as the agent of the id in sanctioning the actions manifest through the ego. It is however quite possible for a seemingly intelligent human to have a weak and vulnerable ego with comparatively limited development. This is most evident in a human's visible susceptibility to the often irrational sanctions (resulting from HAB) imposed by the ego-ideal and the instinctive impulses of the id. This is often manifest by an individual's craving for attention or recognition from fellow humans accompanied by blatant attention seeking. You only have to go into any prestigious university and see the evident backbiting and competition between some of the professors who are supposed to be pinnacles of society's intelligence, but actually show remarkably poorly developed and needy egos. Much of the action of these poor humans certainly shows very little evidence of wisdom as we have defined it.

You can see from this situation the dilemma that my species is now faced with. It is not necessary for a human being to have wisdom in order to survive. In many cases, those most successful at competing in our societies and gaining access to positions of power and influence are often those most susceptible to the passion of their unconscious drivers. The consequences of having knowledge that has developed at a far greater rate than essence within our species may however be bringing us to the brink of extinction, as the vehicles that exist to wreak havoc on each other become more powerful and sophisticated. We are also increasingly wreaking havoc upon our world and the finely balanced natural dynamics of the truly wondrous planet that we inhabit. Humanity is increasingly behaving like a malignant cancer that will ultimately kill off its host with the accompanying destruction of itself.

ORB:- you do not paint a very hopeful picture for your species my friend

I am nothing if not an optimist and I refuse to totally give up on my species. I believe it is probable that we are incapable of evolving in time to avoid our own demise but I refuse to accept that it is impossible. This would in fact be a betrayal of the legacy of those within our historical "wisdom traditions" and other wise beings who have revealed much guidance in the past, often at the cost of their very lives, in order to offer my species the possibility of a different way forward.

ORB:- So why haven't these historical efforts yielded more success?

Why can't you ask me a simple question like, "what time is it" or "do you know how to make cream cakes"?

ORB:- because you are not writing a recipe book here so stop whinging and answer my question!

The simple answer is that it has not been in the interests of the power possessing individuals who dominate our societies for humans to evolve, and that the vast majority of humans are blissfully unaware that they are being so effectively manipulated by natural mechanisms acting within their own psyches.

ORB:- oh come off it. Surely even your unfortunately irrational species must be able to see when they are being blatantly manipulated en-masse?

You really think so? OK, time to go back to the God bit again, or to be more specific, "God faiths" which, as we have previously noted are still influencing the majority of my species in defiance of all objective reason. This is by far the best example of the power of HAB manifest through the ego-ideal to bully and manipulate the ego after the id has firmly latched on to an ideology. This influence is particularly powerful when this ideology is fully sanctioned by the society in which it has become embedded.

It is once again very important to emphasise the need to separate "God faiths" from "Wisdom traditions". After our analysis of the workings of the human psyche we can now make a reasoned argument that "God faiths" amplify the ability of the unconscious through the properties of the ego-ideal to limit the scope of the ego for independent evaluation and rather to bind it through HAB. The described action of God in God faiths on the human species is a virtual parallel to the actions of the ego-ideal upon the ego within a human. It expresses an externally applied desire by a powerful entity to bind and constrain humanity through acts of unquestionable worship and submission. The wisdom traditions on the other hand work with the ego by trying to highlight the slavery of the human psyche to HAB and to help the ego evolve beyond these attachments to achieve "enlightenment". This can in turn be seen as a state where the ego has sufficiently evolved that it can escape from the malign properties of HAB and start to exercise a degree of independent objective reasoning. As has already been emphasised this is not seen as a desirable trait by the majority of those power possessing individuals who wish to manipulate their fellow humans, and for whom those engaged in objective reasoning are an anathema.

In my review of the "God faiths" I am going to initially focus on a religion called Christianity and its most important collection of religious texts known as the Bible. This Bible is particularly significant as the first part, known as the "Old Testament", also directly underpins the second largest human religion, known as Islam. Christianity is the religion that has historically dominated much of my particular culture (I live in a place known as England) and therefore it is perhaps the most familiar to me. I also think it is a manifestation of one of the most serious misconceptions ever adopted by my unfortunate species. I will assert that this "God faith," has by the spurious attachment of the God of the Old Testament to the teachings of a man called Jesus, deliberately usurped the ideas of one of the most important wisdom teachers in human history. I will strongly argue that the creation of this irrational attachment has resulted in an enormous cost to subsequent generations, the result being the confused and contradictory God faith known today as Christianity.

I will be exploring this apparent historical travesty in much greater depth later on but it is important that I separate the most influential religious book underpinning Christianity into its two halves before we proceed. This holy book of Christianity, the Bible, is split into the Old Testament which is all about the Jewish people and their tempestuous relationship with their mostly angry and raging God and the New Testament. The New Testament relates to the life of a human called Jesus although the Christians profess that Jesus was actually the son of the God of the Old Testament. To reinforce this claim they anointed Jesus in their religious texts as Jesus Christ, Christ being a Greek translation of the Hebrew (Jewish language) term messiah. I believe that there is a significant body of evidence that Jesus was from the wisdom tradition of religions and therefore associating his life with the teachings of a God Faith creates enormous difficulties for the followers of Christianity. The Old Testament is all about obedience and retribution from the angry God whilst references to Jesus talks about forgiveness, humility, understanding and compassion.

These are direct contradictions which can be seen in the structure and behaviour of the different types of Christianity. Historically the actions of the established churches would strongly suggest that they are primarily linked to the teachings and practices espoused in the Old Testament with purely lip service paid to the teachings of Jesus. The appalling exploitation and cruelty carried out in God's name makes this abundantly clear. There are however genuine kind and positive humans who also call themselves Christians who actually try to follow Jesus's teachings and have their faith firmly rooted in aspects of the New Testament teachings. Having said this, the good old angry God comes into his own even at the end of the New Testament in a colourful section call "Revelations" where God gets really stuck in to tormenting all the ungrateful humans that have not lived up to his expectations.

Christianity is therefore within its own teachings and structures a self-contradiction. The only way to escape this confusion and contradiction, caused by trying to combine what are in effect two highly contrasting approaches, is for the followers to make a choice. They should either decide to follow the demands placed upon them by the raging God of the Old Testament or alternatively to follow the teachings of Jesus within the context of a wisdom tradition. I shall again return to this dilemma.

The Old Testament, through the complex history surrounding its writing, the evident contradictions in its text, and the evidently malign nature of the creature whose will it is supposed to represent, is a truly fascinating text. The God of the Old Testament is a most wondrous illustration of a raging ego-ideal made manifest in the form of a supreme being that is supposed to dominate the fate of humanity. As previously alluded to, the God of the Old Testament could almost have been deliberately written as an elaborate metaphor for the strained relationship between the ego and HAB manifest through the ego-ideal within humans. Any failure to follow the supposed will of the God is met with the imposition of severe suffering, just as failure to follow the dictates of HAB through the ego-ideal can lead to feelings of guilt, melancholia, or even self-destruction (suicide) in extreme instances.

Before we start having a look at the Bible, it is quite useful to look at a few other religions relying on Gods that are now seen as entirely mythological but were once as closely followed by the peoples indoctrinated by them. Much focus is going to be placed at looking at the formidable character that is God as described in the Old Testament and as we need to separate him from any others I shall designate the title Godot (GOD Old Testament) to him (with apologies to the fascinating play by Samuel Beckett of similar name, any association being purely coincidental).

Amongst the most fascinating were the Gods of ancient Greece, Rome and the Gods of the Norsemen. The myths and fables associated with these Gods are wonderfully entertaining reading as the actions played out by the Gods are a glorious amplification through their powers of the action of humans in these communities. Some clearly represented the powerful impulses of the unconscious and uncontrollable emotions and instinctive drivers in humans; others represented the uncontrollable power of nature. A few illustrative examples of these are:

- Thor, a Norse God amongst whose other attributes represented the action of thunder and lightning.
- Mars, the Roman God of war, worshiped by the military Roman legions.
- Zeus, the Greek God, whose Roman counterpart was Jupiter, the king of the Gods, using the title of a male human hereditary sole ruler also known as a monarch.
- Venus, the Roman Goddess of love, beauty, sex and fertility, represented in the Greeks by the Goddess Aphrodite.

The different peoples who adopted these Gods were all at times extraordinarily successful at warring with others who followed different Gods and building successful empires. These successes were attributed to the action and support of these Gods and failures were often attributed to the fact that these Gods had somehow been displeased. What is interesting is that, in time, all of these cultures ended up adopting other Gods, predominantly Godot.

This leads to a bit of a tricky dilemma for my fellow humans who put their trust in Gods. All of these different cultures obviously achieved their success without any interventions from their Gods and Goddesses which they now disclaim. This is not the same thing as saying that these mythical beings had no influence. Gods are extremely useful to secular rulers when mobilising and manipulating their population. Being in "favour" with the Gods was seen as hugely important, and this association was almost universally, whether unconsciously or deviously, exploited by rulers to further their own ends. One of the most explicit examples of this still exists in England where the monarch is also the head of the "Church of England" or if you like Godot's principle representative. This of course implies "divine authority" for the monarch's decisions giving the monarch considerable additional prestige. That this religious authority is attributed to the monarch of a supposedly rational and modern democracy is, on reflection, utterly bizarre!

I find one aspect about the devotion to Godot by the original people who adopted him even more interesting in that they had very few successes, militarily or otherwise, and during most of their history they were being continually punished for incurring the wrath and disfavour of Godot. It does make you wonder why they continued to worship Godot as he was obviously hopelessly outdone by all the Gods of the other peoples who frequently invaded and who were Godot's "instruments of punishment" for much of these times.

ORB:- I really don't understand, why would anyone worship a God that treated them so appallingly whilst all around them other humans were happily worshiping other Gods that seemed so successful?

This is one of the many strange peculiarities of HAB. It's like another friend of mine who insisted on supporting his football club even when they were so awful that they got relegated out of the main football leagues at one point. When there were so many more successful clubs about, why did he remain so stubbornly loyal to a team who consistently punished him by their dreadful performances? I think the other key factor concerning loyalty to Godot is genuine fear. Many of these people genuinely believed (as do over half the current global population) that Godot actually existed and was directly responsible for punishing them if they stepped out of line. So even though they were often having such a miserable time of things they felt it would get even worse if they actually switched sides. In many cases they actually believed that Godot is the only real God which poses an even more interesting question. Why were all those civilisations who did not apparently believe in Godot at all (therefore believing in no God at all in the minds of Godot's followers as the others Gods supposedly didn't exist) not only not being punished by Godot, but happily building wondrous cities and empires with Godot's implied sanction? This strange logic would have Godot actively rewarding unbelievers whilst frequently raining down misery on those unfortunate enough to worship him. Not much gratitude being shown here is there?

Significant elements of the Old Testament, such as a fundamental part called the Exodus and the creation story in Genesis are believed by some to have been written about 800 years after the described events. This occurred as a deliberate act of propaganda for the people of Judea who were actually prisoners in exile in a place called Babylon. These people were suffering terribly and the hope that Godot might decide to forgive them and set them free was one of the very few hopes that they had left. In actual fact it was another bigger empire, the Persians who ended up setting them free through conquest, although naturally the Judeans had to believe it was all secretly the work of Godot. If it was Godot, he certainly rewarded the Persians well for their efforts as he allowed them to build a really fabulous empire whilst worshiping other Gods which didn't bother him at all. Instead of persecuting the Persians for worshiping false Gods he spent many more centuries focusing most of his efforts in giving the poor Judeans a particularly hard time for not worshiping him well enough!

ORB:- From the perspective of rationality this defies comprehension. I simply don't understand why anyone would worship this Godot when there only ever seems to be a downside.

A very good point but again you are using the perspective of rationality with regard to my truly irrational species. The officers of the religion of worshiping Godot did however have a mechanism to continue to enslave the faithful. This was the threat of the awful punishments that would await them after death if their faith in Godot was to waiver at all. As we shall reveal later, the religion of Islam, which also follows Godot, really builds on the creation of fear within its followers based on the terrible retribution awaiting the unfaithful after death.

ORB:- How can you be punished after death? If you are dead, surely there is nothing to punish?

Aha! Apart from copious evidence of decaying bodies and the like, who says that death is the end? The human id is quite capable of creating a very powerful HAB to the idea that something within it will continue after the death of the body housing it, and that this something might still be able to receive nerve impulses and suffer pain. The great thing about this theory is that, as you are already dead, you can't die again and therefore you can be punished for an eternity, whilst here on earth you can only be made miserable for the span of a lifetime. In the environment of the time through despotic rulers, limited medicine and above all the revenges meted out on humanity by Godot, life could in fact be very miserable and also very short. Godot does also have the ability to give you a really terrific time when you are dead for an eternity, rather than just a great time for just a bit whilst alive like all those Egyptians, Babylonians, Persians, Greeks, Romans etc. with their ruddy great cities and empires.

ORB:- As this is all incredibly unlikely, is there any evidence to support this life after death stuff?

Virtually none, at least none that would appear to stand up to any scientific scrutiny although some would claim to have seen visions of the dead, often referred to as ghosts and many cultures revere or even fear the dead. It is also impossible to absolutely prove that it is not true, just that it is extremely unlikely. I think however you are missing the point here. There are two very good reasons why people could be led to believe that this is true.

The first reason is the fact that death is a very difficult thing to face for a human being, the primary purpose of the ego being to preserve life, and it also raises the very difficult question as to the purpose of life. Can you imagine the human unconscious with all its HAB readily accepting the conclusion that a human life has no intrinsic point beyond the propagation of the species? For human beings this can be an extremely distressing thing to contemplate and therefore there is a huge benefit if the unconscious attaches itself to the concept that life has a purpose beyond death. This belief may actually be virtually essential for the survival of many humans unless there is a very well developed consciousness, ego, which can actually accept this fact, overcome the impulses of HAB and find real value in life itself.

ORB:- Yes I can see that this does make some sense if we reflect on how your psyche is constructed. What is the other reason you alluded to?

It is absolutely in the interests of the civil authorities and the religious officers of Godot related faiths to reinforce this point. Throughout history many unfortunate members of my species have been subjected to the utmost cruelty and deprivation by both the civil rulers of their time and representatives of Godot acting in collusion with these authorities. This enables a greedy few to hoard wealth and power at the expense of the many, a situation still starkly prevalent in many present day societies. This oppression and cruelty creates resentment in those who are mostly subject to its more malign aspects, which could eventually lead to the mass of people rising up in open rebellion. This is however relatively rare and mostly people will put up with appalling injustice without resorting to insurrection.

One of the key historical elements resulting from this capacity in the human psyche to submit to unreasonable imposition and cruelty by the ruling elite is the belief in a life after death. People are told that although life is harsh, if they submit to the dictates of the rulers and Godot's representatives they will go to a wonderful place called heaven when they die. If however they defy the rule of Godot's appointed representatives and the ruler (usually the ruler is also seen as appointed by Godot and therefore a representative of his will) they will go to a really nasty place called hell, which is even worse than the misery they are suffering in life. There is an even harsher aspect to the teachings related to Godot, if one of my fellow humans decides that they have really had enough of the misery of life and decide to kill themselves to escape from its clutches, this will constitute a mortal sin. The act of escaping from your various tormenters will therefore give you a one way ticket to the horrors of hell with no chance of redemption.

You can therefore see why it is very much in the interests of the power possessing individuals who prey and exploit their fellow beings to convince them of the absolute certainty of life after death. It is also very much in the interests of the civil rulers to present themselves as Godot's appointed on earth and reign similar harsh judgements upon their fellow beings in their own interests, emulating the character of Godot himself.

ORB:- What you appear to be saying is that humans are trapped by the properties of HAB, the deliberate manipulations of their historical leaders and the officers of Godot faiths into a kind of perpetual submission. Is there really no way out of this situation? As a rational being I find it beyond any comprehension that your species allow themselves to be so obviously enslaved.

Exactly, my strange species have enslaved ourselves and submissively acquiesce to the manipulations of those amongst us who are probably least interested in our collective welfare. Belief in Godot is just one of the chains that we use to bind ourselves through the unfortunate properties of our psyche although it is one of the most powerful and pervasive ones. The most damaging thing of all is the justification Godot provides as a role model to power possessing humans to carry out appalling acts of persecution, retribution and suppression on fellow beings.

I think it is very important once again to remind ourselves of the extraordinary contradictions within the nature of the religion called Christianity. These contradictions are a direct result of the linking of Godot worship to the teachings of what I will strongly argue was a teacher from the wisdom tradition named Jesus. The followers of Christianity are trapped into a strange conundrum by trying to lead their lives guided by two totally different and largely irreconcilable doctrines. You can see each Christian's faith as somewhere on a scale with Godot at one end and Jesus at the other. The more Godotian they are, the more they seem perfectly happy to sanction discrimination, nationalism, inequality, lack of compassion, narcissism, the right of privilege and the accumulation of staggering wealth at the expense of others in society. The more towards Jesus they are, the more they tend demonstrate behavioural characteristics such as forgiveness, compassion, charity, self-sacrifice and kindness.

I, exercising my rights as the author, intend at this point to make an attempt to fundamentally unravel the split personality of this strange religion. I am going to call those who are mostly influenced by the Godot myth Godotians, and those who are primarily influenced by the wisdom teachings of Jesus as Jesians. I think perhaps we can safely name those firmly stuck in the middle as simply "the confused". Unfortunately for the world in which we currently find ourselves, the vast majority of those who would call themselves Christian are in fact strongly Godotian. This is particularly true in a country called the USA where unequivocal Godotian policies, geared towards the celebration of power and wealth, and harbouring a cold and cynical disregard for the most vulnerable in society are dominant influences in the political sphere. In particular, for what is known as the Republican Party in the USA, belief in Godot, combined with a celebration of vast accumulated personal wealth and the merits of greed and self-interest, is a prerequisite to standing virtually any chance of political office.

Chapter 5 – The God of the Old Testament (Godot) and the human psyche

ORB:- Now just hold on a minute Buzzard. You appear to be undertaking a severe character assassination of this (as you perceive) mythical Godot, but from what you tell me, many of your species seem to follow Godot with genuine passion and adoration. You have presented me absolutely no evidence of the malign qualities of this God faith character. Let me hold you to a higher standard; imagine that you were putting Godot on trial, what would you charge him with? If you can convince me that Godot truly has this damaged psyche, I can then understand why you are so concerned at the role model that he presents for his followers.

As always you are absolutely right, I have allowed my own perceptions and prejudices to run away in my writing and I must therefore go back to the evidence. Before I do so I will however point out that the image and personality of Godot is much misrepresented by the language used to describe him by his believers and the officers of Godot related religions. They use terms like magnificent, glorious and even more incredulously, loving, to describe Godot. This is not surprising if you look at the world at the time that Godot was invented.

The world of my species was ruled by primarily despotic tribal and national leaders with exceptionally needy egos. One word from these leaders could mean tremendous advancement in the eyes of your fellow humans or alternatively disgrace and frequently death. These tribal or national groupings of humans also waged continuous wars with each other over scarce resources or as a matter of prestige. Success in warfare was seen to reflect glory for the whole tribe and therefore HAB to the tribal or national leaders was often extremely strong. It is one of the many calamities that has befallen my unfortunate species that much of this has not changed.

In these types of society, publically espoused love of the leader was not an option but a necessity for continued survival. There was a very recent example in human history that brilliantly makes this point. Recently in a rather strange and isolated country called North Korea, their leader named Kim Jong-il died. His reign was marked by the virtual collapse of the economy, extreme poverty, famine, imprisonment without trial, torture and execution. In any objective sense, the people of North Korea suffered appalling hardship through the actions of this leader and his fellow acolytes in power. At the time of his death however, one million citizens, roughly one twenty fifth of the population, gathered in the central square in the capital and wept profusely at his death. Naturally some of these were there because failure to show remorse was likely to bring severe retribution but I believe many were there because the peculiar properties of HAB meant that they felt a genuine loss and fear for the future. The word prevalently used by these unfortunate being in describing their feelings for this recently demised malevolent character was love, the one thing he had never actually shown to his people.

I think this is a very interesting parallel because the evidence I am going to present about Godot makes Kim Jong-il look like a paragon of virtue. Despite this, throughout all the texts of the Godot religions there is frequent use of the words love, compassion and mercy. Going back to the tribal cultures that invented Godot, if the leader decided to favour you instead of torturing and murdering you, in a strange way you could have considered this an act of compassion. It is compassionate relative to what this despotic leader could have done to you. This is very much what compassion looks like when referring to Godot. Don't forget, if you upset Godot it is not just this life that can become a misery but he can condemn you to misery for an eternity after you have died owing to the cunning wheeze of the life after death bit in the God faiths. I believe that the continued belief in Godot and his role model status for despots has been a significant negative factor to the way our societies have developed and why the evolution of our species seems to have stalled.

I think it is also very important to look at the natural world from the point of view of the people at the time that Godot was invented. There was no notion of the concept of evolution that we can now trace back through the fossil, genealogical and geological record. There was no understanding of different pressure systems in the atmosphere, ocean currents, the jet stream, sun spots and all the other natural factors that can bring drought and death, fertile rains or even calamitous flooding. There was no understanding of plate tectonics and how these can cause fearsome earthquakes, tsunamis and create wondrous mountain ranges when they collide. All that my species knew at this time was that they were in great danger from both their oft tyrannical leaders and the perceived cruelties of the natural world. Life for the peoples of those times was a very tenuous thing indeed. Is it surprising then that they came up with a concept to explain this in the form of a terrible and magnificent being called Godot who had this power of life and death over them as they were so powerless themselves?

The only thing that does inspire incredulity is that the majority of my species still worships Godot despite the incredible advances in scientific knowledge which contradicts so many of the historical teachings of the early Godot faiths. One of the most Godotian of the Christian sects known as Catholicism actually put people to death for having the audacity to say that all the evidence showed the earth went around the sun. As man was made in the image of Godot (one of the key tenets of Godot faiths) and Godot made heaven and the Earth then it made sense that the Earth was the centre of everything and any other theory was heretical! It's a bit of a shame that we now know that the Earth (although I love our small planet and nature with a passion) is an insignificant planet in the outer arm of a relatively minor galaxy in a universe of which there are estimated to be at least 100 billion galaxies. Not quite so significant after all then!

All these ancient peoples had many historical Gods before Godot became so prevalent, many of these being linked to manifestations of nature. There is evidence in the historical record that the Israelites worshiped the God Baal, a god of the rain, thunder, fertility and agriculture, amongst others before their migratory exodus to Egypt. This is why their later texts rail against anyone who made reference to worshiping Baal over Godot when they came back to the land of Canaan. The most important God of the ancient Egyptians was for instance Ra the sun God which kind of makes sense in a primarily desert region where water is one of the most precious commodities and that the great golden orb of the sun dominates all. If I am to be mischievous I would point out that as the Egyptians managed to create an incredible civilisation and in human perception, glorious empire over several millenniums, Ra and the other Gods of Egypt certainly seem to have been a better bet than poor old Godot at the time!

ORB:- well stop being mischievous and enough of this preamble Buzzard, evidence, show me evidence!

Evidence I shall now bring. I shall source my evidence from two of the most influential Godotian texts. The first is the Old Testament, which is based on texts primarily authored by the Judean or Jewish people but as we have discussed is also primary element of the texts used by the religion called Christianity which is still prevalent in my society today. The second is a text called the Koran or Qur'an which, along with the Old Testament, is a sacred book for those following a religion called Islam. The Qur'an is supposed to be an accurate recollection of the revelations made by Godot to a particular human called Mohammed who lived between 570 and 632 CE. The followers of Islam believe that the Qur'an is the unequivocal voice of Godot revealed to them through Mohammed who was known as the Prophet. In the Qur'an Godot is known as Allah. The one key thing about the faithful of all these different Godot based faiths is that their particular texts are to them the absolute word of God and are therefore the unequivocal truth as they see it. We are looking at a formidable manifestation of the power of HAB, particularly when you realise that within these texts are obvious self-contradictions and exceptional contradictions of the historical evidence. I shall come back to this but first let me see what I can come up with in regard to the evidence in respect to Godot's personality.

I firmly believe that the people who originated Godot, and the subsequent generations who wrote the texts that comprise the Old Testament, made God in the image of my own unfortunate human species. As we have previously stated, the world in which they lived was largely outside of their control. They lived in a hostile world. Through forces of nature they were subject to droughts, plagues, famines, floods and earthquakes. In the human world they were subjugated by often ruthless and tyrannical leaders and frequently exposed to external threats from powerful and aggressive tribal neighbours who periodically laid waste through acts of pillage and war. Is it any wonder therefore that the personality of Godot had to even more fearsome and formidable that than of the chiefs, kings, pharaohs or emperors? If we look at the absolute power wielded by these rulers over life and death, is it any wonder that these people believed that the power of Godot to create and destroy had to be much greater still. It can be seen from Godot's personality, as portrayed in the relative religious texts, that he is very much a creation on the human id, instinctively primeval, raging against humanity's weaknesses. Exactly as we would expect from Freud's model of the ego-ideal raging against the human ego.

Let's start at the first text recorded in the Old Testament which for abbreviation I shall now refer to as OT. This is however a moot point as some scholars maintain that this part, which covers the theory of creation, was written much later than some other parts. This first bit of the OT is called Genesis and it relates to two humans called Adam and Eve who were supposedly the original humans made by Godot (yes, I know this would cause significant problems in the gene pool but they didn't know about DNA for goodness sake). Godot created Adam first, supposedly in Godot's likeness and image and then made Eve so that my dear species could start to multiply. This is a bit of a worry already as we know about the peculiar properties of the human psyche and, if Godot has these issues too, we should already rightly be very afraid. Godot gave these two a garden to tend but created this tree, representing the knowledge of good and evil, with strict instructions not to eat of the fruit of the tree or they would die. So God created my species with a thoroughly inquisitive mind and stuck a ruddy great temptation in the middle of the garden knowing full well that this will be irresistible and therefore a great opportunity to start punishing his creations. There is also an interesting subtext to all this, what Godot was actually saying was that he expected my species to remain ignorant and simply obey his commands. This is a key aspect of God faiths as opposed to wisdom traditions in that any attempt to evolve human understanding and challenge the "truths" of the various texts is strictly discouraged. In effect Godot and the God faiths would very much like to hold the evolution of the human psyche at the level of the blessedly ignorant Adam and Eve.

Of course, with the help of a serpent (which we could parallel with the human ego if we were to get all philosophical) they ate of the tree and suddenly became ashamed of their nakedness. In effect Godot (who as I have previously alluded too represents the manifestation of HAB in the id via the ego-ideal in humans) has created shame or original sin as Godotians like to call it and this is the start of Godot's railings against the abject failure of his own creation. There is an even bigger problem here for women as in Genesis we have the start of the Godotian tendency towards misogyny (distaste towards women). According to the OT it was the woman who gave the fruit from the forbidden tree to Adam and therefore Godot decided that childbirth would be extremely painful for women from this point forward and that their husband will rule over them. Godot then basically condemns Adam to a life of toil for his weakness and kicks him out of the Garden. So Godot creates a flawed species, sets them up to fail, creates the concept of guilt, condemns women to be subservient to the male of our species (which seeing as most women I have met are far more perceptive emotionally intelligent than men is a bit rich), condemns human kind to a life of toil and kicks them out into the wilderness. How is the evidence stacking up against this Godot character so far my dear ORB?

ORB:- barely more than a misdemeanour at this point compared to the actions your species gets up to. You will have to do a bit better than this Buzzard.

Fear not, I am just getting started! The next bit is a bit of a misdemeanour too but I can't resist it as it includes one of my very favourite contradictions in the dear OT which we are still expected to believe is the ultimate truth according to the word of Godot. Adam and Eve have two sons called Cain and Abel, Godot favours Abel over Cain so Cain decides to kill his brother in a fit of jealousy. Godot is a bit miffed at this and decides to do the old banishing bit again against Cain. Now comes my really favourite bit. Cain says to Godot, "my punishment is greater than I can bear, I shall be hidden from thy face a fugitive and whoever finds me shall slay me." Do you get it ORB?

ORB:- I think you take far too much pleasure tormenting the writers of this OT, you should reflect on your character Buzzard. Of course I get it; there is supposedly only Adam, Eve and Cain alive at this point so who are the others that are going to do the slaying?

I know, I know, it is actually not the writers of the OT that I am tormenting it is those amongst the current population who choose to suspend rational thought and continue to believe in these myths. Anyway I haven't quite finished yet, dear old Cain is sent off to the land of Nod (though we don't know how a land gets named when there are no people) and knew, a biblical way of saying procreated with, his wife and had a child Enoch. Now where on Earth did she spring up from? Cain then built a city, not something you really need when there are no people about. Yes I admit I am rather enjoying this but there is a far more serious side to this. There is a large percentage of my species to this day that call themselves creationists, ignore millions of examples of scientific evidence about the age of our planet and the evolution of our species and teach that Godot made humans despite the fact that the OT even contradicts itself. Our scientists have recently discovered that many of my species that migrated to parts of a land mass called Europe have approximately 3% of their DNA inherited from another species known as the Neanderthals. Bit difficult for humans to have successfully bred with a separate species without a common ancestor don't you think? Can you see the extraordinary impact that HAB has had to the possibility for evolution for my species?

ORB:- I can see why you have raised this as a very good example as to how HAB can distort human thinking and I am truly alarmed for your species. However this does not really reflect much on the character of Godot so can I ask you to stick to the point. I think one of your Judges would say that this was not relevant to the case relating to your assertion that Godot has a malign character and is a bad role model for humanity.

Argument sustained Milord! I would now like to raise the example of Noah, previously mentioned as it was this very example that suspended my belief in Godot when I was 5 years old. It might be useful to do a bit of a timeline here, according to religious scholars; Adam and Eve were supposed to have been created along with the Earth between about 4000 – 3750 BCE depending on the scholar. This is slightly surprising to us non Godotians as the geological record estimates that the Earth is roughly 4 – 4.5 billion years old. Now according to these scholars, between about 2300 and 2100 BCE, or about 1700 years after the creation of Adam and Eve, Godot decided that his extremely flawed creation was beyond hope apart from a guy called Noah and his family. To rectify his own design flaw, Godot decided to drown every man woman and child on the Earth in a great flood or as we would now call it, he decided to commit an act of almost total genocide. According to the OT, Godot tipped Noah off so that he could build a huge boat to save his family and also a breeding pair of every species on the planet. Bit tricky on the dietary front but apparently no real problem to Noah although you can't help having a bit of sympathy for the poor old polar bears having to be rounded up from an ice floe several thousand miles away to be shipped to a hot and sweaty boat floating on the 31st parallel. Now it is hard to imagine that even the human babies at the time had been so naughty that they deserved to be drowned, rather an extreme form of collective punishment don't you think?

ORB:- I think the case for the prosecution is definitely growing here, Godot creates a species in his own image and then wipes them all out in a petulant tantrum because they don't live up to his expectations.

Except of course he didn't.

ORB:- Make your mind up Buzzard, you just said he did!

Well it rather looks like this was just another example of Godot picking on the poor unfortunates who were unlucky enough to worship him. They seemed to think he had wiped out everyone but Noah, but everywhere else on the planet, where people were worshiping slightly more human friendly Gods, civilisations were bustling away as good as ever. They seemed sadly oblivious to the poor suffering of the people over on Noah's patch. Even next door in Egypt they were happily building pyramids right through this period from 3200 BCE until 1800 BCE and civilisation was thriving. As you may perceive, it is a bit difficult to build pyramids when your workforce has apparently just been drowned by a petulant Godot. In China the Xia dynasty was busy making pottery and developing a thriving culture and in South America at Norte Chico there was evidence on continuing civilisation right through from 3200 BCE until other cultures started to dominate the region from about 1800 BCE. Even more tricky is the evidence that all of these civilisations existed way back before Adam and Eve were supposed to have appeared such as the Yangshao culture in China which dates from approximately 6000 – 5000 BCE or a couple of thousand years before Godot decided to make Adam. So it looks like Godot was being slightly economical with the truth when he told poor old Adam and Eve that they were the only people on the planet. Still, at least it explains why Cain had no problem finding a wife when he popped next door to the land of Nod where there were probably hundreds to choose from.

ORB:- do you have any more evidence for the prosecution?

I have just started my dear friend. We now leap forward on our timeline to an event called the Exodus. Now this is a bit tricky to pin down but some religious scholars have this occurring around 1450 BCE which would have been in the reign of Thutmose III. Others, which seem to reflect the most popular estimate, have the Exodus at around 1250 BCE during the reign of Ramses II otherwise known as the Ramses the Great. After being nearly all drowned, the tribes of Israel (Noah's decedents according to the OT) appear to have had an extremely rapid breeding spree and then followed a colourful character called Joseph to the land of Egypt. They then apparently hung about in Egypt for approximately 400 years. After this period, perhaps because they seem to have been so incredibly successful at multiplying, the Egyptians decided they had become a bit of a burden and the leader, the Pharaoh decided to give them a bit of a hard time. Godot sent a message to a human called Moses to tell him to go to the Pharaoh and tell him to let the Israelites leave with him to a new promised land. The next bit I think really gives us some insight into Godot's character. He tells Moses that he has "hardened the Pharaoh's heart so that he will not listen to you: then I will lay my hand upon Egypt and bring forth my people, the sons of Israel out of Egypt by great acts of judgement."

What Godot is saying here is that, although he could easily have softened the Pharaoh's heart so that when Moses asked if they could all leave he would have said, "fine, off you go" he decided to harden it instead. After hardening the poor Pharaoh's heart so he had no choice but to refuse, Godot used the opportunity to inflict 10 different plagues upon the unfortunate Egyptian people. The last one was to kill the firstborn of every family in Egypt. Godot went around murdering innocent Egyptians en-masse because the Pharaoh refused to obey him, even though Godot had prevented the Pharaoh from obeying him through his own action. This whole escapade was therefore an elaborate farce so that Godot could torture and murder the Egyptians through collective punishment.

This last plague was apparently the last straw and so the Pharaoh suddenly must have had his heart softened enough by Godot to finally tell Moses and the Israelites to clear off. According to the OT the Pharaoh then changed his mind (possible after a quick bit of heart re-hardening by Godot) and chased after Moses and the Israelites with his whole army. Godot then conspired to drown the Pharaoh and his whole army in the Red Sea so that the Israelites could escape.

ORB:- so Godot is adding torture and further mass murders to his previous genocide. I must admit he really is starting to more than compete with some of the worst actions of the tyrannical historical leaders of your own strange species.

Except he probably didn't.

ORB:- Buzzard you are starting to try my patience!

Well once again we hit on a bit of a historical problem. Both Thutmose III (latterly referred to as the Napoleon of Egypt) and Ramses II (the Great) were really spectacularly successful militarily during their reigns, a bit tricky when you have had a third of your population wiped out by the murder of all your firstborns and your army has been completely eliminated through mass drowning. There is also rather mysteriously absolutely no record of these events whatsoever in the extensive contemporary Egyptian records of the time. You think losing the firstborn of every family and the complete annihilation of the nation's army might have been worth the odd hieroglyph or two wouldn't you? In fact the only mention whatsoever of the Israelites is a poem or stele in the time of Ramses's successor Merneptah which states that during a military campaign "Israel is laid waste." Those Egyptians must have learnt from the Israelites post Noah and done an awful amount of rapid breeding to build the army up a bit quick. Joking aside, the real point here is how the authors of the OT actually perceived the nature of the God that they were choosing to worship. You can see why this is not the sort of role model that any wise being would want to develop a religion around. It gives complete license to anyone following Godot to engage in the most appalling atrocities using Godot's nature as a justification and role model. Sadly this is all too frequent even today after thousands of years of history and after society has supposedly evolved.

ORB:- Any more evidence you wish to provide?

I could go on and on because the whole bible is full of Godot's continued retributions. Mostly it has to be said Godot's fury was focused on the poor Israelites themselves who were misguided enough to worship him. They apparently did not worship him nearly enough at times, requiring various extreme forms of punishment to be meter out to them as a means of divine retribution. This is a continued theme but if you think about it there is a real simile here with what it must have been like to be ruled by a cruel and despotic human ruler of these times. It is often the subjects of such a ruler who end up suffering the most, although the carnage inflicted on neighbouring peoples by these disturbed human rulers throughout our bloody history can't be overlooked. By their own texts, worshiping Godot has been a constant affliction to the poor Israeli people which is maybe not so surprising. As previously mentioned, much of the OT was supposed to have been written when the Judean authors were enslaved in the country of Babylon after being thoroughly trounced in military conflict.

There is one more passage in the OT that I will pull out as this is I believe used as an excuse for some really dreadful collective punishment meted out on a long suffering people called the Palestinians. Now naturally after 400 years, the lands from where the tribes of Israel had migrated, quite voluntarily I might add, were settled by other peoples and new cities built. Godot decided that he would hand over this land to his favourites, the tribes of Israel (at least favourites until the next time they decided to cheese Godot off). Despite the fact that this is against any natural law of justice, just conquering these lands and cities was nowhere near enough for Godot. They were ordered by Godot to murder everyone but the residents of just a single household in Jericho, men, women, babes in arms to be slaughtered. They repeated this theme with the City of Ai, murdering everyone but the king. In fact the only city where the inhabitants were basically enslaved rather than murdered was Gibeon. There is a familiar theme going on here. Godot made certain that none of the peoples that came up against his band of murdering thugs were prepared to make peace. Once again Godot decided to "hardened their hearts so that they should come against Israel in battle, in order that they should be utterly destroyed, and receive no mercy". Godot could have softened their hearts so that there could have been a peaceful accommodation but this would have not satisfied Godot's blood lust. Instead there was an open opportunity for raping, pillaging and mass slaughtering to be had after a bit of the old mandatory heart hardening.

Now in my country just under 400 years ago there was a group of people called the Pilgrim Fathers who left Plymouth to create a new colony in what is now in the state of Massachusetts in the USA. This action by Godot and his merry band of sanctioned murderers would be the equivalent of the Pilgrim Fathers after 400 years of breeding and multiplying coming back in a hoard and slaughtering everyone who now lives in Plymouth and the surrounding area because Godot said it was alright. Quite rightly, even our oft comatose United Nations Security Council (an international body whose purpose is amongst other things to attempt and often fail to mitigate some of the potential for mutual slaughtering in my species) might sit up and take notice.

The reason that I have felt it so important to recount the last example from the OT texts is that it gives complete justification for any of the various Godot related religious groups to carry out the most appalling acts against other groups of people. All it takes is for some of the officers of the religion, or an appropriately Godot anointed leader, to state that Godot has sanctioned a course of action, and they can happily suppress all aspects of conscience and wreak appalling misery and havoc on their fellow humans. This type of behaviour is repeated again and again in the history of my disturbed species. Right up until the present day, power possessing humans regularly invoke Godot's name for their acts of systematic cruelty to other human groups. Shia and Sunni Muslims rail against each other even blowing up each other's religious buildings known as mosques. Apparently Godot spoke to George Bush, the President of the USA, a Christian Godotian, before he waged war under the false pretence of non-existent weapons of mass destruction against the country of Iraq. Seems a bit strange that the all-knowing Godot didn't tip old George off that these weapons weren't actually there? The Prime Minister of my own country, Tony Blair, was also a bit equivocal as to whether he also felt that Godot had a hand in his decision making as we too joined in and waged war on the Iraqis. The Roman Catholic Church, a very Godotian orientated Christian sect, in collusion with various despotic rulers, have sponsored countless crusades against other populations in the name of Godot. They even had their own torture squad up until quite recently known as the Inquisition, who went around creating fear and terror in the population to ensure that they were following Godot's will, or at least the Catholic version of his will. As we have already surmised, the probability that Godot exists is virtually nil, but as you can't prove it, and because many people are convinced of his existence through the power of HAB, just about anyone can say that they have been guided by Godot and initiate some or other savage act. The bizarre thing when Christian groups do this is that such behaviour and actions are a direct contradiction of all the recorded teachings of Jesus and would therefore be inconceivable to a Jesian.

In the very same lands that the original slaughter of the Canaanites took place, present day Israeli authorities are waging collective punishment on a poor and marginalised group of people called the Palestinians. My species waged a particularly appalling war known as the Second World War which ended in 1945 CE. Both before and during this war the Jewish people (the decedents of the tribes of Israel in the OT) were deliberately targeted and slaughtered by order of the initiators of the conflict, the German Nazi Party. The complicit acquiescence and often active support of these terrible actions by the wider populations under Nazi influence is one of history's most disturbing examples of the malign qualities of collective HAB. After this conflict in 1947 CE, the United Nations made a decision to partition the land that was known as Palestine. After armed conflict with neighbouring Arab countries, a new state of Israel was established as a home to the Jewish people who had survived these acts of state sponsored genocide under the Nazi's, known as the holocaust.

This decision displaced many of the Palestinian people who inhabited these lands. Even the small areas set aside for them after 1947 have been constantly eroded by successive Israeli Governments through settlement. The intense provocations caused by such acts, exacerbated by the actions of both sides, often leads to exchanges of retribution between them but the one main aspect that is evident to the independent observer is the complete disproportionality of this. In the last conflict starting on 27th December 2008, 13 Israelis died (4 from their own hand known as a friendly fire incident) and estimates of between about 1150 and 1400 Palestinians were killed, bombarded in their captive enclave by a highly sophisticated, largely USA financed Israeli army. This is said to have included by some sources, approximately 400 children.

The excuse for this slaughter was that Israel was "defending itself" but the response and subsequent blockade of Gaza is one of the most appalling examples of collective punishment on a vulnerable people in modern times. This caused barely a stir in the largely Western dominated United Nations Security Council. Now if the Governments of the United States of America or Israel had carried out an action of "self-defence" that meant the loss of 400 of their own children the peoples of these countries would have risen up in absolute outrage against their Governments. These were however children of "another tribe" and what's more, they are living on land that the largely Godotian influenced peoples of these countries believed was left to the Israelis by Godot. As we know, Godot has historically sanctioned the most appalling crimes against those who stand in the way of his chosen people. This legacy from the text of the OT is therefore still having a terrible consequence for the poor civilian Palestinian population who are inconveniently resident in what many Israelis claim as their promised land. The interesting aspect about this is that the Palestinians are also nearly all Godotians through their Muslim faith.

ORB:- I give in, you have supplied more than ample evidence that, if he actually existed, Godot would probably be the most sad but also the most appalling of all creatures!

Well ORB, we have a mental health illness which afflicts some of my species of which sufferers are known as sociopaths or psychopaths. These are potentially very dangerous people who in the majority of cases have to be sectioned (compulsorily detained in a secure mental health institution by power of law) for the safety of other humans. The extraordinarily needy and immature ego, bullying, lack of guilt and remorse, loss of temper and violent acts, air of incredible self-importance and above all the extraordinarily display of narcissism requiring the constant worship of others, would certainly classify Godot as a raging Psychopath. The more worrying thing for humanity is that it is not possible to section Godot and put him away somewhere secure for both his own treatment and for the wider safety of my poor species.

ORB:- So why would any rational being choose to worship such a dreadful character?

Firstly we have already ascertained that I do not belong to a rational species, just a species that may just have the potential to evolve to be rational. The reason so many of my fellow humans are Godotians I believe is fear, and fear is one of the most very powerful human instincts embedded in our unconscious id. Followers of Godot often refer to themselves as God fearing and I believe this is no accident. There is nowhere to hide from an all-powerful ever present psychopath like Godot, just like it was very difficult for the long suffering subjects at the time when Godot was conceived to escape from the retribution of the despots who dominated their existences. These people had two basic choices, obey or perish and the human instinct for survival is very powerful. If you combine the enormous power of HAB to make emotional attachments to external influences, and combine this with the instinct of fear, it is perhaps less surprising that even today; the current majority of my species defy all rationality to follow Godotian orientated religions. My anxiety is of course that there is very little possibility for my species to evolve unless the powerful collective HAB to Godot inherent in my species can be broken. This will only happen if the majority of my species choose of their own volition to follow the path of rationality. This is, I firmly believe, the objective of the wisdom traditions throughout the ages.

Before I move on to look at the wisdom traditions I think it is useful to look a little bit more at how Godotian religions have used fear to ensnare followers. There is ample evidence of this in the OT but I think the more recent Godotian religion of Islam and in particular the text of their holiest book, the Qur'an (sometimes known as the Koran) is particularly revealing.

ORB:- The evidence of Godot's fearful character as espoused in the OT will be hard to beat. What is it in the Qur'an that can further increase the fears of your poor misguided species?

Aha, this goes back to what we discussed earlier, the most cunning manipulation of all by the Godotian religions, what may happen to you after you die. This is the potential misery that you may have to endure, not just for a lifetime but for an eternity should you not choose to flatter Godot's immature and needy ego. Sit back and listen to some of these examples but first a little bit of history about the Qur'an to put this text in context with the OT.

The Qur'an was written between 610 and 632CE in what is now Saudi Arabia and is to Muslims the unequivocal word of Godot as revealed to the prophet Muhammad. The evidence in the Qur'an is virtually pure OT or possibly from more traditional common texts from which the OT was also derived. The Muslims believe that all the words in the Qur'an were transmitted directly to Muhammad through revelation. The great similarities of the historical examples cited in the Qur'an to Judean texts and the lack of any real pertinent historical reference to Godot beyond these texts leads the dear old cynical Buzzard to suspect that Muhammad most probably had some original Judean scrolls. The result of this is that all the contradictions we have already highlighted with historical evidence about the origins of humanity, Noah's flood, the Exodus etc. are also replicated in the text of the Qur'an. What can be truly said is that Muhammad certainly had his own particular take on some of the stories from the OT.

During the time the Qur'an was written there were local tribal conflicts going on between Muhammad's people and the citizens of the city of Mecca. The peoples of this time were believed by some scholars to be polytheists, believing in a number of Gods of which Allah, Islam's name for Godot was just one. The attraction of following one powerful God was a useful rallying point for the different tribes that Muhammad was trying to unite against the people of Mecca and therefore quite attractive in HAB terms. As we have previously discussed, combining tribal leadership with the additional HAB of religious belief creates a very powerful bond in the human psyche.

Muhammad's main complaint with the Israelites was that they were by no means submissive enough to the wrath of Godot so he goes to extraordinary lengths to explain the dire consequences awaiting the unfaithful in the afterlife. In the Qur'an, belief in Godot and his prophet was absolutely everything and the actual act of a believer choosing to leave the faith was punishable by death. It is a sad fact that some strict observers of Islam still put people to death for this even in our modern times. Severe retribution is still very much characteristic of the strictest adherents to Islam, which are often called fundamentalists. Beatings, dismemberments, executions, and torture are very much in vogue (Godot could only applaud) within many of the regimes although to be fair these are also prevalent in many non-Islamic societies.

The dear old so called bastion of the free world, the United States recently re-introduced torture although the weasely wordsmiths within the US Government called these "enhanced interrogation techniques." The ability for the US Government "spin doctors" to use wordplay to excuse appalling behaviour never ceases to amaze me. During recent years they indulged heavily in kidnap, imprisonment without trial and sponsored torture through third part agents. They call this "extraordinary rendition" knowing full well that nobody would have a clue what they were on about. They also indulge in summary execution without trial (targeted killing) and the systematic violation of international borders to kill other nationals using primarily unmanned killing aircraft known as drones or UAVs. Interestingly they only do this to people of other tribes and nationalities; if they ever did the same thing to an American (at least one on American soil), a democratic western ally or one of their Israeli buddies there would be a huge public outcry. Good old US Godotians! I can just imagine the Americans response if someone flew a UAV over America and started bumping off American citizens. The extraordinary myopia and hypocrisy of this nation is simply staggering at times. It would be interesting ORB, if you were to decide at some point in the future to return and observe whether my species has developed any evidence of evolving. A first positive clue you might be inclined to look for would be if humans were observably treating every man, woman and child on the planet with the same concern regardless of ethnicity, tribal loyalty or nationality. We have a huge evolutionary journey to make as a species if we are to reach this point.

ORB:- Buzzard, as is so often your way, you are straying from the point again.

Please accept my apologies my dear friend. The Islamic type of Godotian religion is also extremely patriarchal and women in most Islamic societies do not share equal rights to their male counterparts under religious or sharia law. This can cause significant tensions when these communities are embedded within more secular democratic societies, a consequence of recent human migration and the multi-cultural societies that are now prevalent in the modern world.

Nearly every chapter or sura in the Qur'an starts with "In the name of God (as in Godot), the Lord of Mercy, the Giver of Mercy". This is extremely significant and illustrative of a Godotian religion; it becomes quite apparent that there is only mercy available to those who unequivocally worship Godot. For everyone else Godot's imagination in conjuring up horrific tortures has only probably been exceeded by the most tragic and debase tyrants characterising the unfortunate history of my species. The advantage Godot has is that he can inflict misery for an eternity whilst all too often, to the disappointment of human torturers everywhere, human victims have a tendency to eventually die from their abuses and thus ending their entertainment prematurely.

Here are just a few examples of Godot's ingenuity in the creation of suffering from the suras of the Qur'an:

"Garments of fire will be tailored for those who disbelieve; scalding water will be poured over their heads, melting their insides as well as their skins; there will be iron crooks to restrain them; whenever, in their anguish, they try to escape, they

will be pushed back in and told, taste the suffering of the fire". Not a particularly inviting prospect.

"As for those who defy God, their home will be the fire. Whenever they try to escape it, they will be driven back into it, and they will be told, 'taste the torment of the fire, which you persistently denied". There is an interesting link to this particular fate in that the Prophet who states that he and his followers will *"make them taste a nearer torment prior to the greater torment (Godot's) so that perhaps they may return (to the right path)"*. What this is implying is that Godot's followers will take it in hand to create misery for those who refuse to believe whilst alive. The strange rationality of this approach is the hope that the threat of violence will intimidate them into becoming believers, doing them a favour so as to spare them from Godot's even worse torments. This is an ingenious sort of "heads you lose, tails you lose even more" proposition which was also very much favoured by the Catholic Inquisition.

After telling his followers what a wonderful time they will have in paradise he further warns; *"Is this the better welcome or the tree of the Zaqqum, which we have made a test for evildoers (non-believers). This tree grows in the heart of the blazing fire, and its fruits are like devils heads. They will fill their bellies eating from it; then drink a scalding mixture on top of it; then return to the blazing fire"*.

These are but a few of the examples, throughout the pages of the Qur'an are constant themes of eternal punishment in the fire, torment, retribution, there really seems to be no end to the revenge that Godot can mete out on those who defy him or refuse to believe. Being a Godotian is to live in constant fear of the wrath of Godot.

One of the aspects about the Qur'an that does intrigue me is Muhammad's vision of what paradise is like. *"God's true servants. They will have familiar provisions – fruits – and will be honoured in gardens of delight; seated on couches, facing one another. A drink will be passed around among them from a flowing spring: white, delicious to those who taste it, causing no headiness or* intoxication. With them will be spouses – modest of gaze and beautiful of eye – like protected eggs."

More on this theme; *"We pair them with beautiful-eyed maidens; we unite the believers with their offspring who follow them in faith – we do not deny them any of the rewards for their deeds …… we provide them with any fruit or meat they desire. They pass around a cup which does not lead to any idle talk or sin. Devoted youths like hidden pearls wait on them."*

What we have in the Qur'an is exactly the same deal offered by Godot in eternity as the despotic rulers at the time could offer in life. Disobey (disbelieve) and you will be condemned mutilated and horribly tortured, obey (believe) and you will be granted a hedonistic paradise. It's no wonder that rulers usually end up being surrounded by sycophants with this deal and it seems that Godot in heaven is no different. It is also interesting to note that hell is always likened to fire and heat whilst heaven is linked with cool water, fruits and drink. I think this is very revealing of the hot desert climate prevalent in the region of my planet where the incidents in the Qur'an took place. Water in these regions is a rare and precious commodity whilst there is also the fierce heat of the sun and the parched dryness of the desert. It is therefore little wonder that these particular concepts of heaven and hell were created to bribe or threaten the faithful.

In the part of the world where I live we get so much rain that the outside of the houses go green with the growing algae. The main worry about the streams is that they may swell so much in the heavier downpours that they can flood our houses. Sitting next to a stream on soft cushions is therefore possibly not the ideal vision of heaven in my part of the planet. Sitting on a deckchair in the shade of a hot sun sipping a cocktail might be slightly more alluring but as they say, "different strokes for different folks".

Paradise would however be very short lived! With any understanding of humans it would be understood that after a relatively short time, all these faithful who had ended up in the garden next to these streams, sitting on cushions, surrounded by maidens and youths and drinking these wonderful drinks would get seriously bored! After a few weeks or months, let alone an eternity, they would be looking for other distractions, start squabbling amongst themselves over who should have which maiden, and probably end up incurring the wrath of Godot anyway for being so ungrateful. Ultimately I suspect we will all end up in Godot's fire one way or another!

The Qur'an gives concluding evidence of the appalling nature of Godot and how he rages against those who refuse to worship him, punishing my species for an eternity to satisfy his unquenchable bloodlust for vengeance against us poor defenceless inferior little beings. I'm still not quite sure why Godot would want to be worshipped by such a weak and feckless species as I would have thought that this would do little to assuage his rampaging needy ego but there you are.

As an aside it is also again interesting to note the highly patriarchal nature of Islam as there is much reference to the joys for the menfolk on death being paired up with beautiful virgins. What is noticeably absent is any reference of what's in it for the women, except for the small matter of avoiding being burnt alive for an eternity. I believe, just as in the OT, this implicit implication of the supposed inferiority of women has had a hugely detrimental and unforgivable impact upon the rights of women through the ages. It is only in very recent times and only in certain communities that women are finally getting the respect and emancipation that should always have been their basic human right.

Well now my dear ORB, how do you find the defendant Godot? Is he guilty or not guilty of being a dangerous psychopath in desperate need of urgent medical attention?

ORB:- Oh without doubt guilty as charged, but actually most guilty of being a poor creature almost totally driven by instinctive passions and the unconscious rages of his ego-ideal. He shows evidence of great insecurity and loneliness and of having a very needy embryonic ego with a lack of any cohesive rationality. This is not a creature to be judged, this is a creature to be pitied. The frightening thing is that we can be relaxed about Godot as a mythical construct but extremely concerned for your species that invented such a creature and are now burdened with continued belief through the malign influence of HAB. It is small wonder that the history of your species is riddled with examples of conflict and hatred both within and between various identifiable groups with Godot as a role model.

Thank you for your concern, you can see why I am so passionate that we try to understand the impact that HAB has on my species and how it has impacted upon my species' ability to evolve. I also think you have hit on an extremely important point. The descriptions of Godot in the OT and the Qur'an actually reflect a being that is at the very lowest levels of evolution of the psyche, far less developed than many humans. This, if they could just see it, is the biggest clue to the huge numbers of my species living in fear of the wrath of Godot that Godot is indeed a myth. In every example where humans have successfully developed their psyche and escaped the more extreme entrapments of HAB, the personality developed by such humans is a complete contrast to the personality assigned to Godot. Development of understanding universally leads to humility, compassion, love, forgiveness and a desire to assist and create harmony amongst fellow beings. These more developed members of my species know that anger, hate and greed actually act against the development of a mature ego and an associated peace of mind. It is basically impossible to act like Godot after having acquired wisdom. The big question that I truly request followers of Godot to consider is how is it possible that the whole of the universe, the world, humankind and the plants and animals of our beautiful planet were created by a being who is palpably less wise than most examples of the human species? Any being with the understanding to create the universe would be a complete opposite to the petulant, narcissistic, insecure creature evidenced in Godot or to put it even more simply, how is it that humans were created by an even more inferior being than the majority our own troubled selves? The only sensible answer is that they weren't and that Godot was a necessary creation to explain a world that seemed so frightening and out of control which we now understand so much more about.

As I said in the introduction to this book, it really is time that my species escaped from such primitive notions. I would say childish notions but this would be really disparaging to many of our children. They would never make such attachments to Godot through their HAB without the intensive programming of their collective ids by their parents and the societies in which they are embedded. This last point concerns me more than any other at this time. The only hope for evolution of our species is through our children. Even in my society which is supposed to be science based, rational, modern, liberal and democratic, the current Government is actually encouraging Godotion based religions to take over many of our schools. Programming our children with Godotian concepts is surely the one crime against our future generations that we should prevent at all costs. If our children choose to learn about Godotian religions and decide through freedom of choice to follow them then this is their right. Actually deliberately programming children, knowing how HAB will develop around such a process and that they will create highly resilient bonds to such notions is unforgivable. Do we really want our next generation to develop behaviour patterns using Godot as a role model?

Chapter 6 – The wisdom tradition and the contradictions in Christianity

ORB:- Could you explain a bit more about Christianity. You state that Christians can be more or less influenced by Godot depending on the different sects they belong to and their own temperaments. It is clear that the Qur'an sends out one very clear if somewhat unpalatable message, believe in and worship Godot or burn in the fire, but I am still confused as to how Christianity can be both Godotian and yet as you insist, also a wisdom tradition? Can you explain what you mean by this and how it came about?

I would be delighted to, but you will have to bear with me on this as the answer is not straightforward.

ORB:- Why does this not surprise me!

I do believe the answer to this question brings some small hope for my species and bizarrely, even for some of the more Jesian orientated churches (as in followers of the wisdom of Jesus) as opposed to the irreconcilably Godotian based churches. The root of the problem goes right back to the very beginnings of the Christian church. I believe what occurred has been the most appalling travesty to the memory of the man called Jesus and the great sacrifice that he made in his attempt to pass on wisdom to my species. The consequences of the actions of some of those in the early Christian church, through no deliberate evil intent I must add, have in my belief had a significant detrimental impact upon the ability of my unfortunate species to evolve.

Before I attempt to answer your question on Christianity I think it is time that I explain in far more detail what I mean about wisdom, the wisdom traditions, and why I believe that these teachings could assist my species to develop an approach for evolving. As I have previously mentioned, I believe that wisdom is a combination of two factors, information or knowledge and essence. Information is fairly self-explanatory and this is something that we have in abundance in our modern age of communication. With the development of the internet and digital technologies most of my species can have access to a virtually inexhaustible amount of information about our planet, our biology, the universe etc. It is not remotely possible for any human to process even a fraction of the information available in their lifetime. Of course there is another problem with all of this in that information can at times be ambiguous, misleading or even downright wrong. Look at all the contradictory information we found just looking into the nature of Godot and the probability of his existence. In order to process information we need another factor which I shall call essence as I can't at the moment think of a better word.

I am going to go back to the convenient Freudian based model of the psyche that I have used to try to make sense of the strange behaviour of my most peculiar of species. We have noted that instinct and the emotional attachments made to people, objects and ideas are formed in the unconscious id. The id seeks to place constraints on the action of the conscious ego through the properties of the ego-ideal. When someone is born, the ego is also very embryonic and struggles to create any understanding of the world around it, a vital necessity if the being is going to survive and thrive. As previously stated, there is only a certain need for the conscious aspect of the human psyche to grow to a certain extent to enable a reasonable chance of survival. Development beyond this point is not essential for survival but is essential if a human wishes to escape from the domination of HAB and instinctive human impulses. This further development of the ego, enabling an awareness of its slavery to different unconscious impulses manifesting themselves in the form of desires, aversions, irrational attachments and fear, is the development of what I would call essence. The more that this potential in the psyche to develop the conscious ego is realised within a human being, the more rational will be the being's evaluation of sources of information. It is this interpretation of information in the context of rationality that I refer to in my ramblings as wisdom.

I would just like to take an opportunity to point out that I make no personal claim to wisdom but I do have an admiration for those humans throughout the ages in which the presence of wisdom was clearly apparent. It is to my sorrow that I do not believe that wisdom is commonly manifested in my species.

Lamentably, rationality as a property of the human psyche is not understood, valued or respected. It is also not in the interest of those in positions of power for the population to develop such a property in their collective psyche. This perhaps explains why the Government in my country is deliberately transferring control of many of our schools to Godotian based religious organisations. Wise people are notoriously difficult to manipulate and therefore unsusceptible to Government spin and propaganda. It is one of my greatest hopes that the recent virtual collapse of our greed based self-interested extreme capitalist system, may in part be the wakeup call that my species requires to realise that they need to build a more rational future if they are to survive and thrive.

ORB:- So what you are saying is that a wisdom tradition is one that helps a human develop the ego beyond the grip of the restraining bonds of HAB and the instinctive emotions, and realise a greater human potential.

Got it in a nutshell! I believe that actively seeking wisdom creates the potential for my species to further evolve rather than regress but I am extremely doubtful as to whether this will ever come to pass. It will require a very different society and a huge collective effort to get there and unfortunately apathy and inertia are very prevalent properties in my species.

Anyway, let me draw on some evidence of what I believe are positive examples of wisdom teachings through the ages before I use this analysis to address the vexed question of the evolution of the current model of Christianity.

Firstly I think it is very important to tackle the word God in relation to wisdom traditions. This term is frequently used but is nothing like the personality based rampaging entity depicted by Godot. The concept of God in the wisdom traditions is so different that I am going to have to use a different word other than God to prevent the obvious risk of confusion. The relationship between humans and the conception of God in the wisdom traditions is not a two way personal relationship such as that which is supposed to take place between Godotians and Godot. It is a relationship between a person and their own developmental journey towards a developing knowledge of the nature of things. The majority of the wisdom traditions I shall refer to state that "God is unknowable" in any conventional sense by a human being. Realisation of the nature of things, that is to say realisation of God, is achieved through a process of prolonged personal struggle against the unconscious instincts and desires that so dominate our psyches, leading to a state of enlightenment. In the context of this book this can be paralleled with a person's struggle to escape the effects of their HAB.

This essential path towards a greater understanding of the reality of things was very aptly put by a very wise Hindu sage living in India called Ramana Maharshi to a visitor who enquired as to the nature of God. These are a few extracts from the conversation recorded in the Teachings of Ramana Maharshi by Arthur Osborne:

Disciple: "God is described as manifest and unmanifest. As the former, He is said to include the world as a part of His Being. If that is so, we, as part of the world should find it easy to know Him in His manifested form."

RM: "Know yourself before you seek to know the nature of God and the world."

A bit later in the conversation:

Disciple: "But is it not necessary to understand His nature before one surrenders oneself?"

RM: "If you believe that God will do all the things that you want Him to do, then surrender yourself to Him. Otherwise let God alone and know yourself."

This gets very much to the crux of the matter with regard to wisdom teachings. My thoroughly conceited species believes that they can try to understand God when they don't even understand themselves. We cannot even observe and understand the unconscious influences and irrationalities that so dominate our own consciousness. What Ramana Maharshi is basically saying is that if you want to understand the nature of God and the world in which we live you first need to understand yourself. Understanding is a function of wisdom and wisdom has to be worked for. If, as the God faiths universally demand, you want to hand over your responsibility for yourself to whatever notion of God you may have then go ahead. This should however not be confused with trying to understand the nature of the truth of things which begins with work on oneself.

This is why so many people are open to manipulation by the unscrupulous amongst my species who hold positions of power and influence. As the God faiths demand that you surrender yourself to God, without of course understanding the nature of God because you can't even observe the manipulations of HAB on yourself, you need an interpreter. This creates a hierarchy of officers of the different religions who will tell you, trying to be one of the faithful what God is saying. These vast religious hierarchies are highly likely to be comprised of unenlightened beings who also do not understand the nature of themselves let alone God. Many amongst their number will also be harbouring conspicuously needy egos within their psyches which will significantly influences their behaviour and the genuine motivation behind it. This leaves vast numbers of my species being actively and deliberately misled to meet the interests of the power possessing individuals within the religions that they submit to. The faithful can be told almost anything by the officers of their religions and this carries the implicit authority of God in their role as the interpreter of God's will. The devotees are absolutely none the wiser as to whether there is any truth whatsoever in what they are being told. Their religious obligation is to "have faith" that what they are being told is in their interests and is true. Sadly, it is exactly this submissive unquestioning obedience that those who desire to manipulate human populations wish to create. As we have previously discussed, the pursuit of wisdom is the last thing that most political, civil and the God faith based religious leaders wish to encourage.

As previously stated, God in the wisdom tradition is not an identifiable being such as Godot but a supreme universal spirit, known in Hindu teachings as Brahman. The Gnostics actually thought that Godot (who they called the Demiurge) and the world he dominates was a product of a schism in the absolute. Godot was a barrier for man who has the divine spark (also referred to in Hinduism as the Atman) of the absolute or universal spirit within him and struggles to realise his divine nature and become re-united with the universal being. In Gnostic belief, Godot wishes to manipulate humanity for his own ends and prevent my species realising its ultimate destiny through reunification with the universal spirit. This would repair the schism in the absolute and recreate divine harmony. This human path towards realising their divine nature is achieved with the help of Sophia (divine wisdom). This Gnostic perspective does have some interesting parallels with what we have already discussed in relation to the importance of developing wisdom to help escape from the manipulations of HAB. It is also no coincidence, given what we have discussed of the properties of HAB, that in Buddhism, attachment is seen as the root of all suffering. Transcending the grip of attachment in Buddhist teachings is an essential path to the liberation of the human spirit or achieving a state of nirvana.

Gandhi in his autobiography has explained this far better and more simply than I have to date. Gandhi, known to his followers as "Mahatma" (or great soul) much to his embarrassment, was an extraordinarily enlightened human who lived in India during the twentieth century. Gandhi led a nonviolent movement against the iniquities of British rule in India and was sadly assassinated for his courage. In his autobiography, Gandhi states that "my uniform experience has convinced me that there is no other God than Truth" and that "the only means for the realization of the truth is Ahimsa" (nonviolence). This is the absolute core of the wisdom traditions; the path to God is work on oneself to unpeel the layers of illusion that envelop us and reveal the ultimate truth of things. God and truth are therefore synonymous and their nature starts to be revealed through a process of rigorous enquiry. This is a completely opposite approach to the blind faith and submission required by God faiths.

We can now see the dilemma of using the term God, a term used by both the wisdom traditions and the God faiths that mean two virtually polar opposite concepts. Gods like Godot are beings of emotions, anger, petulance, narcissism and vengeance, in other words entirely human-like in concept. The God of the wisdom tradition is the absolute, the unknowable, universal harmony and to re-quote Gandhi, the ultimate truth. The only path to knowledge of God in a wisdom tradition is through first gaining knowledge of one's own self.

In many ways, the path of science relentlessly unlocking the secrets of the universe, including the very building blocks of life, is complementary to the objectives of the wisdom tradition. Science aims to change our concept and understanding of the universe around us, just as the wisdom traditions endeavour to overcome the illusions that inhibit the evolution of the human psyche. The eminent physicist and atheist Stephen Hawking said in his book a brief history on time: "However, if we discover a complete theory, it should in time be understandable by everyone, not just by a few scientists. Then we shall all, philosophers, scientists and just ordinary people, be able to take part in the discussion of the question of why it is that we and the universe exist. If we find the answer to that, it would be the ultimate triumph of human reason - for then we should know the mind of God." This statement is entirely compatible with the objectives of the wisdom traditions who also attempt to free humanity from the illusions created in the human psyche to reveal the truth of things.

I would go so far that both science and wisdom are equally necessary for the evolution of my species because as I have warned so often before, information without wisdom can be exceedingly dangerous and we are very capable of destroying ourselves as a species. Information and technological development, in the hands of a human who has not overcome the constraints of HAB, such as someone addicted to personal greed or a God faith based fundamentalist who believes that they know the will of God, can rapidly lead to calamity. Unfortunately for my species the lessons of the wisdom traditions are not embedded in the societies that we have created and this has, and continues to cause great suffering for our poor species. On the other hand, the development of an essence within a human being without information, also places limitations on wisdom and the ability to apply wisdom proactively in our world.

I have been absolutely fascinated by the arguments that are raised, largely by Godotians that science has not disproved the existence of God when there is no universal understanding of what is meant by the term God anyway. The differences between a God faith depiction of God and a wisdom tradition concept of God are immense. Wisdom tradition concept of God being the ultimate manifestation of the truth and science's quest to understand the nature of things are entirely compatible. The assertion that everything in the universe was made by a being like Godot 6,000 years ago is alien to both science and wisdom traditions alike.

ORB:- What you appear to be saying is that the term God is essentially highly confusing as it can mean completely different things to your species?

Indeed, there is nothing like language to confuse a dialog. Just as I have found it necessary to create the terms God faiths and wisdom traditions to try to eliminate much of the confusion around the term religion I think it is necessary to do the same with the term God.

ORB:- so what do you suggest?

Well, as this is my conversation I shall use the term "the universal nature of things" to describe God as I have such a passion for the manifestations of nature on my planet and the majesty of the universe in which it is embedded. The extraordinary beauty of nature and the plants and animals populating my small planet are the closest thing I get to a feeling of spirituality, or what the dear old Gnostics might say, in touch with a spark of the absolute. As "the universal nature of things" is a bit of a mouthful I shall call what I understand to be the God of the wisdom traditions as the Unot. The Unot is not to be confused with Godot, Thor, Odin, Zeus or any other incarnation cast in the human mould which I shall continue to call Gods.

ORB:- So to be clear, you propose that we have God faiths with their Gods, and wisdom traditions with their search for an understanding of the Unot?

Exactly, although of course this term is completely alien to everyone outside the context of this conversation. The great thing about the Unot is that the scientists can also join in on the journey without fear of contradiction although they are generally focused on rather different aspects of the Unot.

ORB:- Have you any more examples as to how the wisdom traditions characterise the Unot?

Well don't forget that in the wisdom traditions the search for the Unot is commenced with trying to understand the true nature of the self or the human entity. Perhaps true nature is the wrong term here. It is the potential nature for humanity that can be realised through rigorous self-observation and work on resisting the powerful urges and irrational connections made by HAB. For most humans this completely different nature of understanding will never be realised as they will not and indeed have no desire to follow the necessary path towards self-realisation.

There is a wonderful Hindu scripture called the Bhagavad Gita which is a great favourite of mine and was also thought of as a pivotal scripture by Mahatma Gandhi. The Gita is probably set between 1000 and 700 BCE. The setting is the eve of a great battle in a civil war set in India. The Gita relays a conversation between Prince Arjuna and his charioteer Sri Krishna who is a manifestation of Brahman, or as I have interpreted Brahman, a manifestation of the Unot. The battle in the Gita is a metaphor for the battle that Arjuna must have with himself in order to overcome illusion and realise the truth. In effect a manifestation of the Unot through the character of Sri Krishna is helping Arjuna to discover the nature of the Unot within himself, or what is described in the Gita as the war within.

I intend to use some of the wonderful enlightening examples and instructions for human evolution from a wisdom tradition perspective in the Gita. Before I do this there is again the potential for confusion to reign through common language. Both Hindu and Buddhist texts have a different meaning by the use of the word ego from the model that we have already discussed and this requires clarification. Much emphasis is placed on overcoming the ego as Krishna warns Arjuna. "The senses are higher than the body, the mind is higher than the senses; above the mind is the intellect, and above the intellect is the Atman" (the divine spark within humans that enables them to become enlightened and one with Brahman or as I would describe Brahman, the Unot). "Thus knowing that which is supreme, let the Atman rule the ego. Use you mighty arms to slay the fierce enemy that is selfish desire."

This text from the Gita is extraordinarily enlightening and I find it humbling that wisdom that is 3000 years old is still so pertinent today. In the reference to the human psyche in the Gita there are parallels with the Freudian model that I have chosen to assist me in explaining the strange psyche of my species. The mind in the model of the Gita is, I believe, what Freud describes as the unconscious id. This is manifest on the actions of the human through the function of the ego-ideal, the properties of instinctive programming, and HAB. The intellect, representing the ego uses information from the senses to try to make sense of the world and instigate action based on the external context. The intellect or ego in our model is also subject to the drives and imperatives of the unconscious acting upon it via the ego-ideal. The Atman is a concept of a being fully liberated from attachment and desires. The closest representation in the model I have to the Atman is the concept of a fully matured and evolved ego that has escaped the attachments and impulses of the unconscious and makes truly rational detached judgements. The concept of the Atman also has a spiritual dimension which is beyond my comprehension as I admit to being a fully flawed human much dominated by the properties of my emotions and HAB. I do however believe that developing a fully independent ego would be a very necessary pre-condition if a human was to become one with the Atman and understand the Unot. I therefore believe that the term ego as used in the scriptures refers to the properties and attachments of the id manifest through the ego-ideal and not the ego as described in the model I have used. Ego in the model I am using is most closely compared to the development of the intellect as referred to in the verse from the Gita.

ORB:- So for ego in the scriptures read id, manifest through the properties of the ego-ideal and for intellect in the scriptures read ego. The full development of the intellect would be a pre-condition to becoming one with the internal manifestation of Brahman (the Unot), which is the Atman. I think I get that.

Thanks for that ORB and I do realise for many that these may be truly unfamiliar concepts. The main point from all this is that wisdom cannot be achieved without escaping from the properties of HAB and the human instincts embedded in the id. Overcoming these influences emanating from the human unconscious is a truly formidable struggle for any human. The first step on the path to wisdom is for a human to accept that they have nothing approaching an independent will. It is to start observing the manifestation of emotions and attachments that result in fear, aversion and desire in their everyday lives. It is like being on a sailing ship, one cannot fully avoid the actions of the wind, but through observation you can watch its impact on your vessel and mitigate its effects though thoughtful adjustment of the sails and the tiller. To maintain the metaphor, most of us deny the existence of the wind or pretend that we are immune to its effects and we wonder why both as individuals and as societies we so frequently end up wrecked on the rocks.

Here are just a few extracts from verses in the Gita that are particularly relevant to the limitations placed on the human psyche by HAB and the resulting desires that so influence a human being.

Sri Krishna:

"Those who are motivated only by desire for the fruits of action are miserable, for they are constantly anxious about the results of what they do……..The wise unify their consciousness and abandon attachment to the fruits of action."

In answer to a question by Arjuna about the nature of those who live in wisdom; *"they live in wisdom who see themselves in all and all in them, who have renounced every selfish desire and sense craving tormenting the heart. Neither agitated by grief nor hankering after pleasure, they live free from lust and fear and anger. Fettered no more by selfish attachment, they are neither elated by good fortune nor depressed by bad, such are the seers"*

The following is especially pertinent to a later exploration of the miseries of the extreme capitalist model and greed that currently pervades in many cultures; *"attachment breeds desire, the lust of possessions that burns to anger. Anger clouds the judgement; you can no longer learn from past mistakes. Lost is the power to choose between what is wise and what is unwise, and your life is utter waste."* I think that this extract from the Gita shows that the wisdom and understanding of human nature 3000 years ago is still absolutely relevant to the modern age. If we look at how greed and attachment in those running the financial markets has led to what has effectively been the virtual bankruptcy of most of the world's leading economies, we can see the truth of these words. Greed and attachment and the lust for possessions resulted in a complete lack of the power to choose wisely and learn from past mistakes and only bitterness, despair, and resentment amongst peoples was ultimately realised.

Here are some other words of wisdom that may give us some useful insight should my species decide, however unlikely that is, to build their future societies on mutual responsibility instead of greed and self-interest. *"Strive constantly to serve the welfare of the world; by devotion to selfless work one attains the supreme goal of life. Do you work with the welfare of others always in mind……The ignorant work for their own profit Arjuna; the wise work for the welfare of the world, without thought for themselves…..perform all work carefully, guided by compassion."* Indeed Sri Krishna is even more explicit about the impossibility of those focused on selfish desire to gain knowledge and wisdom; *"knowledge is hidden by selfish desire, hidden, Arjuna, by this unquenchable fire for self-satisfaction, the inveterate enemy of the wise."* It is with the greatest sorrow that I observe the country of India, the birthplace of such wisdom, also adopting the most nefarious aspects of the viral capitalism that has infected western societies with such tragic consequences. Inequality in India is increasing exponentially; more billionaires are being created at a frightening pace whilst extremes of poverty ravage the majority of the people. As we have already proven in most Western economies and Japan, this is a completely unsustainable model of capitalism that will ultimately lead to civil unrest and financial collapse. These warning signs are also very evident in other developing economies like China, Russia and in South America. It gives me a significant sense of shame, living as I do in the UK, that the so called Anglo-Saxon model of extreme socially irresponsible capitalism is infecting so many other societies in our world. The writers of the Bhagavad Gita would I am sure despair how little my misguided species has learnt since their words of wisdom were first drafted 3000 years ago.

ORB: Buzzard, you have made an interesting point here. Are you saying that the same wisdom that applies to development of wisdom in individuals can also apply to the creation of wise societies?

I am absolutely convinced of it. I firmly believe that the actions required to create a wise human have close parallels with the actions required to create wise societies. As societies, we make irrational attachments to objects of desire, are often inward looking, self-interested and negligent of the needs of others. How easy it is for those who indulge in manipulation of the masses to whip up the worst aspects of nationalism thereby creating insecurity, collective violence and hostility between identifiable different groups. We have already alluded to this when looking at how identifiable differences between the Godotian sects can lead to appalling examples of collective violence when the spectre of fear and insecurity is raised in the collective psyche of the faithful. It is not beyond the realms of analysis to look for the id, the ego-ideal and the ego operating within society as well as within an individual human. The irrationalities within us as individuals are often manifested in the irrationalities we see in the societies around us.

I think that this is also a clue as to why, despite thousands of years of the existence of wisdom traditions, that my species has evolved so little. It is not possible for many amongst a population to work on their psyches to the point that they have acquired significant levels of wisdom. Most of the wisdom traditions, quite understandably, focus on the development of the self as a pre-requisite to the building of an effective society. I can remember reading a passage from one of the books written by G.I.Gurdjieff where he put forward the idea that wisdom was material and finite like every other commodity and that there was not enough to go-around. Fortunately he said, only very few in the world are actively seeking it and therefore it is quite possible for individuals to gain wisdom when the vast mass of humanity remained blissfully ignorant. I can't say that I fully endorse this theory but it would certainly go some way to explaining the world in which we live. Greed, desire and self-interest within society will always be given the opportunity to reign supreme unless active measures are taken to mitigate its excesses. This would require a degree of wisdom from those in position of power and influence. Unfortunately the genuinely wise are unlikely to give in to such desires and attain these two obvious manifestations of HAB, as they actively feed the appetites of the unconscious vanities that act against any desire to develop a rational ego.

All too often societies can distort the teachings of wisdom traditions to meet the aims of self-interested groups, much to the detriment of others. There are for instance parts of the Hindu scriptures that refer to following one's dharma which can be equated to following the natural law of the Unot. There is also a belief in some wisdom traditions in reincarnation, this is said to occur if a human does not reach a state of enlightenment and has to work through the consequences of their actions during their lives. These traditions believe in the law of Karma which says that every action sets off a chain of consequences. Actions undertaken with compassion and positive intent generate positive karma and actions that are selfish and gain advantage at the expense of others create negative karma. This karma is worked out both in this life and through the next life, so if you have been disharmonious to your fellow humans you are likely to be born into a hard life and if positive and harmonious, into a good life. Generating positive Karma is therfore conducive to reaching the ultimate goal of enlightenment (or as I would say, escaping the clutches of HAB).

These principles have however historically been, I believe, misused in Hindu society to develop a system of different castes. This system can result in segregation and discrimination between humans as it is based on the belief that whichever strata of society a human was born into is a result of previous karma and it is therefore your dharma to stay in this class without any scope for social progression. This is completely against the wisdom of compassion, understanding, humility and selfless work in the interests of others. It feeds attachment, self-interest and discrimination. Fortunately the India of today, is working actively to try to eliminate such discrimination and bigotry between its citizens. I absolutely share Gandhi's view that such a system is a perversion of the messages of the wisdom teachers in Indian history. I only use this example to show how easily societies can adopt corrosive practices that can become an established culture supporting vested interest and feeding the worse aspects of the collective psyche. Greed and self-interest at the expense of others can grow very quickly and at great cost. Anyone but the very privileged living in Greece, Ireland, Portugal, Italy and Spain, amongst the countries worst affected by the collapse of the global financial market, can tell you this first hand.

There are other examples such as the demands for large dowries from female brides and extravagant weddings that are obvious attachments to materialism and vanity that also appear to be completely contrary to the teachings of the

Bhagavad Gita. These are direct results of cultural distortions that enable the powerful and rich to display their social standing to others in society. All this really displays is the power of HAB in these individuals to make attachments to materialism. This has become such a distortion within some in Indian society that female babies are actually identified and aborted in the womb or killed at birth in order to avoid the cost of meeting these perverse cultural expectations. Can you imagine how Brahman, the Unot, in the form of Krishna would view such behaviour if he was looking down on contemporary Hindu society manifest by these examples? To re-quote from earlier to just try to get the point across *"attachment breeds desire, the lust of possessions that burns to anger. Anger clouds the judgement; you can no longer learn from past mistakes. Lost is the power to choose between what is wise and what is unwise, and your life is utter waste."* Those who indulge these cultural practices and material attachments, in the words of the Gita itself, are leading towards lives of utter waste. This distortion of Hindu teaching does however pale into complete insignificance if we look at how the world in the Christian sphere has betrayed virtually every single teaching of the wisdom teacher named Jesus who supposedly initiated their religion.

ORB:- Just before you move on, what are your thoughts on reincarnation as expressed in Hinduism, Buddhism and other related wisdom traditions?

I personally find it very difficult to believe in such a notion because I have no evidence to support the proposition that there is an imperishable aspect of the human psyche that transcends death. I have however already admitted that I am rather a cynical old git and therefore defer to those of a more spiritual nature on such matters. I have great respect for many of the words of guidance towards wisdom by the teachers of old so I have to accept that they must have had some good reason to have faith in this concept. It is however very hard to comprehend when you see the deterioration of both the body and the mind, especially in cases of Alzheimer's and dementia that there is something intrinsic of the entity left behind. This is to be honest a bit of a relief seeing as how, according to the different Godotian sects, the vast majority of us are going to be tortured by Godot or his appointed minions for an eternity. If I am right in my beliefs, Godot wouldn't have much left to persecute after we have shuffled off our mortal coil as William Shakespeare so eloquently wrote in Hamlet.

I did think about this a bit in the past but actually came to quite a logical conclusion that it actually didn't really matter. I thought about what sort of life I would like to lead in order to be relatively positive to my fellow beings and try to follow what small vestiges of wisdom I managed to accrue. Would my approach to life change if I knew I might be reincarnated? I decided that it wouldn't actually change anything because if you are only trying to lead a positive life through fear of the life to come then you are actually following the path of self-interest and have not come to this through the path of rational realisation. This unfortunately is only therefore another manifestation of HAB and contrary to the path of the personal development of a mature ego. So my advice is to try to lead a positive life for the right reasons, not because of some expectation of reward based on insincere action.

Another reason why I think it doesn't matter too much is that for the vast majority of us, we have absolutely no recollection of any past existence so we have no option but to play the cards that life has dealt us, whether these are the result of past life karma or not.

ORB:- you said a bit about certain characteristics that are common to all wisdom traditions with an objective to realise the Unot. Could you give me some further examples of this before we return to the perplexing theme of Christianity?

Thank you for this question dear ORB. I intend to make the case that Jesus was in fact a teacher of a wisdom tradition, rather than an aspect of a God faith Godotian based religion. If I am to build this case I need to supply much more evidence of what is manifest in a wisdom tradition. The overpowering logic underpinning this is that any tradition that offers a path to seeking the truth or the Unot is always likely to gravitate towards the same point. There is after all only one Unot and although I have said that it is beyond the ability of the vast majority of my species to know the Unot (leaving the possibility for enlightenment in the very few). It is therefore entirely logical that some of the key understandings of the different wisdom traditions start to align as you come closer to the prize.

I previously mentioned that the Buddha stated that attachment, to which he added anger and ignorance were causes of suffering. This parallels my instincts about why understanding and overcoming the more pernicious aspects of HAB is so important. It is also our first clue of many to come, as to why the Godotian faiths are unlikely to bring about an end to suffering. They require us to follow an **angry** God, remain in **ignorance** and rely on an **attachment** to faith accepting the holy texts as the absolute truth. We have already discussed in detail the efforts that God faiths make to ensure that HAB makes a strong bond of emotional attachment within the faithful, starting with the intense indoctrination of children. In short we have every essential element in a Godotian tradition to create suffering within my poor species. Contrast this with this quote attributed to the Buddha (many thanks to the wonderful website, viewonbuddhism.org by Rudy Harderwijk):

"Do not accept any of my words on faith, believing them just because I said them. Be like an analyst buying gold, who cuts, burns, and critically examines his product for authenticity. Only accept what passes the test by proving useful and beneficial in your life."

It is easy to see that this wisdom tradition searching for the Unot sends the completely opposite message to a God faith. I also love this quote from the 14th Dalai Lama *"Don't try to use what you learn from Buddhism to be a Buddhist; use it to be a better whatever-you-already-are."* This is emphasising the importance of self-work and self-inquiry in order to develop as a human being rather than being attached to a prescribed set of ideas.

I think that the quote from the Buddha also has a much wider lesson for contemporary society. It is a serious flaw in our human psyche, originating with the identification made within the ego-ideal that we put great faith in who it is that says something rather than trying to understand what has been said, and whether it makes sense. You could have the most enlightened being contact the media, a politician or publish something on a website and absolutely nothing will come of this contact unless they are famous or accredited to have a valuable opinion, such as being a professor in the subject. The very last thing an enlightened human would want to do would be to feed his or her vanity by seeking fame! The most complete idiocy is often blithely accepted without question if it comes from an approved source.

One classic example of this was the credit rating agencies who up until the very last minute were putting "buy" ratings on investments like collateralized debt obligations or CDOs linked to virtually worthless mortgage debt known as "sub-prime" (more deliberately weasely words that nobody properly understood from the dear old USA). You had economists from esteemed universities writing glorious praise of the Icelandic banking system just before it completely crashed virtually bankrupting the poor Icelanders who had nothing to do with this madness. These bastions of academia also somehow forgot to mention that they were being paid lavishly by the same Icelandic financial institutions that they were praising. If everyone took the Buddha's advice and stopped to question whether any of this made sense rather than just looking at who said it, we would live in a very different world. This attachment and identification to individuals extends to the strange breed of humanity, usually with exceptionally needy egos, called celebrities whose every word and gesture is followed by the media. The fame of these individuals combined with the strange workings of the human psyche give their utterances a credibility that is usually completely at odds with the rationality of what is said.

This is underlined even more explicitly by this further quote from the Buddha:

"Rely on the teaching, not on the person;
Rely on the meaning, not on the words;
Rely on the definitive meaning, not on the provisional;
Rely on your wisdom mind, not on your ordinary mind."

The last statement is very important as it shows the explicit importance of developing what I previously referred to as essence or a mind that is resistant to the influences of unconscious impulses and attachments. This puts the information that is being processed by the human into a different context. It underlines the important difference between the gathering of information and the interpretation of information by a person with wisdom (essence and knowledge). Those trading CDOs in the financial markets were very clever and had lots of information. They were however also dominated by a multitude of attachments such as making money, career progression, making a name for themselves and fear of losing their jobs by not following the trend. There is very little evidence that these people ever considered the consequences and the impact that they were going to have on everyone else. Certainly a lot of ignorance and attachment going on here and these actions created a great deal of anger. These factors have created all the necessary ingredients for tremendous suffering amongst my fellow humans, literally in their hundreds of millions if not billions. Again I find it very humbling that this wisdom from the time of Buddha 2500 years ago is so directly pertinent to today's world and isn't it equally sad that in all this time we do not appear to have learnt anything as a species? I sometimes have to pick myself up from falling into despair about the prospects for humanity to ever evolve.

ORB:- Come on Buzzard, stop feeling sorry for yourself and tell me more about how we would recognise a wisdom tradition. What characteristics would you see from someone who was trying to understand the Unot using a wisdom path?

Sorry, but in my defence it is not easy being a human you know! Remaining with a Buddhist perspective the Buddha gave guidance on the correct attitudes and actions to develop on the path to wisdom with the "Eight fold noble path". These are:

1. **Correct view or understanding**: develop genuine wisdom and use wisdom to guide your thoughts rather than impulses and passions
2. **Correct motivation or intention**: avoid attachment to the desire for possessions and jealousy of the possessions of others. Avoid any line of thought that is initiated by hatred or anger towards other people and a wish to cause harm. Be mindful of the consequences of your proposed actions and the negative impact that this could have on others (CDO traders take note!).

3. **Correct speech**: avoid deliberately lying, idle or malicious gossip, cruel or abusive speech that is indifferent to the feelings of others
4. **Correct action**: avoid violence, stealing or any other action that may cause deliberate harm to others.
5. **Correct livelihood:** try to make a living that is consistent with the attitudes to having a correct view, intention, speech and action. Avoid any occupation for your own benefit that overtly harms others as a consequence.
6. **7. and 8. Correct effort, mindfulness and concentration,** these are all disciplines for the development of a permanent embedded wisdom emphasising the need for constant attention.

The final three paths are a very important aspect because wisdom and essence are not easily attained and it is very easy for new attachments, impulses or powerful instincts to permeate back into the ego and reverse the process of ego maturation. I may have implied earlier that the maturation of the ego is a one-way process but this is far from the truth. It is only maintained through applying a consistency of purpose. This is also particularly true when we later come to the topic of building wise societies, these will require constant vigilance as vested interests, the greedy and the selfish will be constantly trying to breakdown any established safeguards. The recent massive deregulation of the financial markets, caused by the intensive lobbying of vested interests, and resulting in catastrophic market failure, is a classic example of what can be expected.

In an attempt to answer the question as to what defines the characteristics of those following a wisdom path, the first and foremost difficulty encountered is being able to actively seek them out. Avoiding attachments and vanities, the wise are unlikely to be found amongst the ranks of politicians or celebrities or, as in the case of the Dalai Lama, they may be reluctantly in the limelight owing to a wider moral obligation. Their ambitions are manifest internally to work on the self, the search for truth and the development of wisdom rather than to seek the accolade or recognition of others. Their actions will be considerate of the needs of others and they will have an evident capacity for kindness and compassion towards other humans and all living beings that share our planet.

ORB:- Buzzard, you briefly mentioned the word moral when you talked of the Dalai Lama and this is a word that intrigues me. What do mean by this word?

Oh my goodness, you have caught me out, this is a word that I have studiously tried to avoid up until now but perhaps it is now the right time in our discussion to have a look at this word and I shall expand this dialogue to look at the words good and evil at the same time. These words are also useful to again differentiate between God faiths and in particular the Godot based religions and the wisdom traditions.

Morality is in most of the sphere of human activity an entirely subjective word. If you were a Godotian for instance, morality is whatever you can glean from the religious texts to be in line with the intentions of Godot. Some of these are on the face of it quite positive such as you shall not kill and you shall not steal etc. The big problem with this is that Godot follows none of these commandments himself and the ultimate morality is to follow the will of Godot. This produces wonderful contradictions such as the Israelites who were supposedly following the commandments, killing every man woman and child in most of the cities in Canaan and stealing all their possessions and livestock. This is equally evident in the different Godotian sects such as the Catholic Church instigating the murder of all the Cathars in the Languedoc in France in 1208 CE, an act of supreme brutality known as the Albigensian Crusade.

It is estimated that approximately 500,000 men women and children were massacred in the Languedoc during the Albigensian Crusade at the instigation of the so called Christian church in the name of Godot. This was justified because the beliefs of the Cathars were not in line with the established teachings of the Catholic Church. Far more importantly, the nefarious creatures who were leaders in both the French Court and the Catholic Church felt that the Cathar religion could be seen as a potential popular threat to their own vested interests and power base. This gives you the Godotian problem with morality; it is whatever those who want to interpret the "will of Godot" says it is at any given time, depending on their particular agenda. This is a real problem with Godotian based faiths; their followers can on a whim be incited to the most appalling atrocities by the various clergy and associated civic rulers in the name of Godot.

As we know, Godot makes a wonderful role model for those wishing to wreak havoc on my poor species.

Other historical examples of Godotian inspired carnage were the crusades in both the Holy Land (Israel and parts of what is now Syria) and Northern Europe in the lands comprising the Baltic states, parts of Russia and Germany. In 1099 after laying siege to Jerusalem, Christ's soldiers slaughtered thousands of men women and children in the name of Godot after taking the city. Tales of the time talk of the Crusader's (Christ's Roman Catholic Church sponsored warriors) wading ankle deep in the blood. Can you imagine how Jesus would have felt to be associated with such horrific crimes of genocide against fellow humans? In the Northern European Crusades, frequent incursions by civil leaders for the purpose of profit and acquisition were blessed by the Pope because the victims of these frequent aggressions were pagan. In return for "spreading Christianity" at the point of a sword and undoubtedly a cut in the proceeds, Godot's representatives on earth gave Godot's sanction for the political rulers to invade and plunder foreign lands for their own selfish purposes. Now why is it I missed the bit in the New Testament where Jesus must have said, "and anyone who chooses not to hear my message will be mercilessly slaughtered in the name of Godot," who, we are expected to believe, is the God of love and mercy?

At the current time amongst my unfortunate species, thousands of men women and children are still murdered, maimed or tortured by what are known as fundamentalist religious groups that in the majority of cases claim to be following the will of Godot. Most of their victims perversely are also fellow Godotians but ones that may follow a different sect or just choose to defy the murderous intentions of various misguided clergy and their devotees.

We therefore have a situation where morality is for the majority of my species a purely subjective term that is completely governed by self-interest and the wishes of Godot by those who appoint themselves to interpret him. The same can be said of good and evil, good is what furthers my interest or follows Godot's current will and evil is what is against my interest or contradicts the current will of Godot. Equally a capitalist can see a day as being very good if he or she can make a massive profit trading in the global financial markets at the cost of a business, country or currency. It can hardly be said to have been a good day using more objective moral criteria for defining these terms.

ORB:- OK Buzzard, what are these objective moral criteria?

I would like to take you back to the wisdom tradition and the objective to be free from attachments and follow thoughts and actions akin to the eightfold noble path. In this tradition good are those intentions and actions that enable an aspirant to escape from the desires and passions of attachment and to undertake a path that will bring a sense of inner harmony. In fact I very much like the word harmony and disharmony as these are far better words that good and evil. In wisdom terms, a moral person tries to bring harmony both within and without with due consideration with their developing knowledge of the Unot. This actively discourages any actions whose results are likely to deliberately create disharmony or harm to others.

This is by no means a simple and straightforward task, which is why the path to wisdom takes long attention and practice. For example, if you were a regulator who imposed restrictions on excessive greed in the global markets, this could be seen by those who seek to profit from those markets as very disharmonious to their intentions. The wise regulator would however understand that the attachments to materialism within these greedy humans were actually damaging to their own psyche and development and that the consequence of their action to their fellow humans was very damaging and disharmonious. In effect, these humans would be creating what the Hindus and Buddhists would consider to be very negative karma for themselves. It can therefore be seen that such action by a regulator would on balance be harmonious, even though it reduced profits for the few. We could use the term good or moral in an objective sense instead of the word harmonious but I would not recommend this owing to the baggage attached to these words historically.

If we are to look towards what kind of society we wish to build with an objective positive morality we should therefore look towards one that promotes both internal and external harmony, and try to avoid one that actively creates disharmony and a hostile environment to individual development. This will be by no means easy as the world is an extremely complex place and it will therefore be impossible to predict all the consequences of actions taken to build a harmonious society. There will be much trial and error but the application of wisdom and consistent intention has great potential over the longer term. This is however very unlikely to take place, as the vast majority of my species will have no desire whatsoever to break their attachments to selfishness, vanity, self-promotion or their cravings for hoarding personal wealth. The fact that these attachments ultimately make most of them thoroughly miserable is unlikely to be considered attractive or persuasive enough to instigate a change in direction. Very few addicts will thank you if you try to protect them from their next fix.

ORB:- You are getting cynical again my friend, I suspect you are far from a state of inner harmony and are somewhat lacking in wisdom! So what you are saying is that an objective morality is that which seeks to promote both the conditions for humans to evolve wisdom and consequent internal harmony, and also the conditions for a wise society or external harmony?

Let your words be of warning to the reader, this discourse is not being written down by one blessed with wisdom, just one who admires it in others and sees its potential to help my troubled species evolve. You have however summarised my argument for objective morality succinctly.

ORB:- Are we now in a position to look at the vexed question of Christianity and the obvious absurdities and contradictions that you have alluded to?

Yes indeed, let me proceed with my argument that the teachings of Jesus were hijacked and attached to the Godot, with whatever good intentions at the time, by practicing Godotians who were previously followers of the Jewish Godotian faith. This is the original Godotian faith, although it naturally has to this day its feuding sects within it, each claiming to know the will of Godot better than the others. Humans will be humans after all. It preceded the Christian based Godotian sects or Islamic based Godotian sects.

First a little bit of background information. Jesus was a human being who was born about 2000 years ago and originated the CE or Common Era calendar, known most commonly as AD or Anno Domini which means in the year of our Lord. This system was devised by the Romans in the year 525 CE who were the dominant empire at the time and were Christian Godotions. The somewhat interesting anecdote relating to this is that most modern scholars believe that the Romans got this wrong and that Jesus was born about 4 BCE or 4 years before his official birth if you see what I mean, all a bit confusing. I think this is very important to understand, the Romans adopted Christianity for the supposed power of Godot within the religion and not for the teachings of a wisdom teacher named Jesus. You can see from the majority of the actions of the Roman Empire that these definitely did not pass the wisdom test to promote the harmony of the Unot.

The Romans adopted Christianity through the actions of the one who was to become the Emperor Constantine I at the battle of Milvian Bridge in 312 CE. It is reported that he saw a vision of a cross before the battle and ordered his soldiers to adorn their shields with Christian symbols. After having duly won the battle with supposedly Godot's help (as we shall see, Jesus was not one for promoting and supporting mass slaughter by his favourites on the battlefield) Constantine legitimised Christian worship within the Roman Empire and ultimately became a Christian Emperor. This started a tradition where it was the position of the Christian Emperor, directly responsible to Godot, to ensure that Godot was worshiped throughout the empire and that the doctrines dictated by the officers of the church were obeyed. This as we have already mentioned with reference to the Albigensian Crusade amongst countless other examples, was often done on pain of death or at least imprisonment and torture. This situation continued throughout most of the next 2 millennia under various Holy Roman Empires which ultimately expired in 1806 during the Napoleonic Wars. It was only at this time that the much despised Holy Inquisition, the Catholic Pope's personal anti-heresy squad using torture and burning as optional extras, finally faded from power and influence. The majority of Catholic Popes were very much made in Godot's image (or is this the other way around, sometimes I confuse myself).

ORB:- Now you are starting to confuse me too, where exactly does Jesus come into all this? You have yet to raise any evidence of a wisdom tradition but instead have succumbed to your usual temptation to rail against Godotians. Is this perhaps a focus for your own particular HAB Buzzard? Can we please get back on track, how did Christianity originate prior to its adoption by Constantine?

My apologies, I suspect you are spot on when you identify that my aversion to God faiths is a product of my own HAB and I warn you that I will undoubtedly succumb again. I do not apologise profusely for this for as you know I believe that the God faiths and Godotian faiths in particular have been one of the most significant factors in stopping my poor species from evolving.

Naturally I cannot tell you first-hand about what Jesus was like so I must like all others draw upon the historical record and various texts to try to develop a picture of his character and look for clues as to the meaning of his teachings. The main established sources about the life and teachings of Jesus are the Gospels of Mark, Mathew, Luke and John, with the majority of scholars having the belief that Mark was the first. These are all in the New Testament along with letters from Paul, a later convert to Christianity and highly influential in the early church. This is significant as we shall discuss later.

It was relatively late in my life that I actually started to get more interested in the life of Jesus. As stated earlier, I discounted the notion of Godot when I was 5 and as Jesus was supposed to be entwined with Godot I felt that there was very little point in delving much further. Like most children I was systematically exposed to some of the parables at school when I was younger and the impression that I got was one of examples showing kindness to others and consideration but little more than that. This message is completely corrupted and overshadowed because of the Godotian aspects of retribution, sin, hellfire and damnation, emphasised by the different Christian churches and sects to a greater and lesser degree. This contradiction in message has always seemed quite bizarre, how can you teach compassion love and kindness and retribution, rage and eternal punishment at the same time? There was a huge clue here that was screaming out to be understood, you can't! The messages are completely incompatible which should have told me at the time that this was probably a partnership of convenience to vested interests. There is no contradiction promoting a relationship with the message of love and kindness and trying to understand the nature of the Unot. As we have seen, consideration of the needs of others and being ever mindful of the consequences of one's actions are key themes running through the wisdom traditions.

There is remarkably little written in the contemporary record about Jesus with just two brief mentions in the works of Flavius Josephus, a historian whose works were first written about 93 CE. One of these messages at least is questioned as to its authenticity as a possible later insertion by the Christian Church. It is not until the second century that references to the Gospels are made and there is a robust debate as to when these were written. There is general agreement that Mark was written first with an earliest date of about 70CE owing to references to the destruction of the Temple in Jerusalem which was known to have occurred around this time. Mark's Gospel is generally agreed to be followed in chronological order by Mathew and Luke with John written from about 90CE as an earliest estimate. There is however also a body of opinion that suggests that none of the Gospels were written until the 2nd century CE. The letters of Paul to the various early Christian communities were written from about 50 CE although Paul himself had no first-hand knowledge of Jesus. He was however in contact with disciples of Jesus who founded the early church. There is some school of thought that the Gospel of Mark was written by a person called John Mark who wrote it in Greek and was influenced and knew Paul. This would correlate to the earlier date of 70CE for the setting down of Mark's Gospel. I personally believe that this was significant as I believe that Paul's beliefs significantly influenced Mark when he was writing the Gospel.

Mark, Mathew and Luke are what are known as the Synoptic Gospels as they are all related, overlapping in content and it is again generally agreed that Mathew and Luke drew heavily on Mark's Gospel when developing their own. There is a significant source of opinion that Mathew and Luke based their Gospels on Mark and another source text or texts that is known simply as Q which is the first letter of the German word Quelle, meaning source. The existence of Q has been deduced from the fact that there is such similarity to the additional material in Mathew and Luke that does not come from Mark that the coincidence is simply too great for this to have come from separate sources.

This actually simplifies things a bit because if we want to ascertain anything about the teachings and character of Jesus without too much additional human interpretation, influencing and church propaganda. We can basically look at the Gospel of Mark (influenced by the thoughts of Paul) and what has been deducted as Q from Mathew and Luke.

Now all this is very well and good but as I previously mentioned I had no desire to read the New Testament in any detail as I was less than convinced that Jesus even existed. As already stated, the references in the historical record from contemporary society at the time, and particularly in Flavius Josephus's history are very few. Certainly at the time it appeared that Jesus was not a significant figure with regard to the civic Roman authorities who had far more active Jewish figures fermenting rebellion against the Roman occupation to consider.

In contrast to my lack of interest in the bible, predominantly to the linkage with the concept of Godot, I did develop an increasing interest in Buddhism and Hindu. I became aware of the concepts of self-development and inner harmony with the world through the writings of Ramana Marharshi as recorded by Arthur Osborne, and from influential texts such as those included within the Bhagavad Gita. I was also influenced by some of the ideas of a philosopher name G.I.Gurdjieff to whom I have made previous reference. In short I was interested in trying to get some idea as to whether there was any evidence of any purpose in life beyond biological reproduction for the human species and naturally a sense of direction and purpose for myself. I openly confess I did not understand much of what I had read at the time and this is still very much an on-going mission. My readings did however leave me with a sense of some of the essence of what I now refer to as wisdom traditions.

My whole attitude to Jesus completely changed when I came across the Gospel of Thomas (GoT). The GoT was found amongst a collection of predominantly Gnostic texts near the village of Nag Hammadi in Egypt in December 1945. Again there is no record of when the texts were originally laid down but what is evident is that they do not appear to be influenced by any of the Gospels and this may indicate that it predated them. The GoT consists of 113 sayings of Jesus that are stated as "These are the secret sayings that the living Jesus spoke and Didymos Judas Thomas recorded." Thomas was one of Jesus's disciples often referred to as "doubting Thomas" which is very significant as I shall soon explain. There were actually 114 sayings found at Nag Hammadi but the 114th is so out of character with the rest that it is the opinion of many, including me, that it was added to the list by a later author for their own purposes. I have therefore discounted saying 114 and stick with my assertion that 113 are from an early original source.

The thing that immediately grasped me about the GoT was that it only makes sense from the perspective of looking at it as a wisdom tradition and makes virtually no sense at all from the perspective of a Godot based God faith. The sayings in the GoT offer a path that is the polar opposite of the blind faith and devotion to Godot that is characteristic of the Old Testament and the other Godotian faiths.

This to me was a clue with extraordinary ramifications for the whole later development and contradiction within Christianity. If Jesus was a wisdom teacher then the whole exercise of linking Jesus's sayings with the Old Testament, and the rampaging vengeful narcissist that is Godot, falls completely apart. Even more importantly it releases what I have earlier referred to as the Jesian part of Christianity from the irrational shackles of Godotian belief. I believe this creates the most extraordinary opportunity to completely re-energise Christians who are predominantly influenced by Jesus and not Godot. They would, to avoid inevitable confusion, have to rename their church as Christianity is irreconcilably associated with the 2000 years of cruelty and infamous acts in its historical baggage. I shall call these potential followers of a wisdom based Jesus, free from the shadow of Godot, as "Jesians" just to be consistent with my earlier description.

This revelation completely altered my view about Jesus, as many of the sayings in Thomas that are not in the Gospels show an understanding of the Unot that could only have come from a very wise individual. It was evident that Jesus had largely escaped from the restraints on his psyche of the more malevolent properties of HAB. It became quite apparent to me that the GoT was a series of sayings that gave firm clues to others also seeking to understand the truth of things. The person of Jesus, if he was indeed as asserted the source of the sayings in the GoT, had suddenly become extremely interesting to me. After reading GoT I am convinced that the 113 sayings did indeed come from a single cohesive source as the language and themes are entirely consistent with this proposition.

ORB:- Let me be absolutely clear about this Buzzard. What you are asserting, after becoming familiar with the GoT, that the whole tenet of Christianity has been based on a fundamental misinterpretation of the teachings and character of the figure Jesus. This is unlikely to make you many friends amongst the hundreds of millions of followers who have very powerful HAB to the current model of Christianity. Are you seriously saying after 2000 years of faith that these people have all been seriously misled? This is a very serious assertion to make as the implication for your species will have been immense.

Yes, this is exactly what I am saying. I think that this gives many of these followers who have been struggling to come to terms with a relationship between Godot and Jesus, liberation from fear, guilt, retribution, the concept of original sin, and all the other baggage which comes with a fear based God faith as promoted by the Godotians. I personally think that this is a wonderful message of hope for potential Jesians as I believe that Jesus was actually promoting self-development and the creation of an understanding and relationship with the Unot.

Chapter 7 – Evidence that Jesus was a teacher in the wisdom tradition and the implications of this for the future of Christianity

ORB:- OK Buzzard, make your case.

Well my dear ORB, we have already discussed some of the principle original source materials available to us. The Gospel of Mark, likely to have been heavily influenced by Paul's teachings and ideas, the deduced source document Q, which supplied additional material for the synoptic Gospels of Mathew and Luke, and the Gospel of Thomas. Thomas was not included in the original Church texts which were, as an aside, the texts politically approved by the Bishops embedded in the Roman Empire in 325CE at the Council of Nicaea, at the behest of the Emperor Constantine. As we know that Constantine was a full blown Godotian, even if the GoT had been known of at the time, it would never have been approved by the church authorities. The Gospel of John was written considerably later than the other Gospels and appears to be more a work of contemporary church propaganda rather than an authoritative recollection of Jesus's teachings.

It is very interesting to note that neither Q nor Thomas make any reference whatsoever to the resurrection which has become one of the key tenets of Christianity. This is mentioned very briefly in Mark where reference in made that Jesus's tomb was empty and that he showed himself to Mary Magdalene, who did not recognise him at first, then to two disciples who told the others but they did not believe them and then briefly to all eleven where he apparently chided them for their unbelief. It is I think of great interest that this supposedly incredibly important event in Christianity is completely missed out from Thomas and Q and only mentioned very briefly in Mark, almost as an add on to the story of Jesus at the end of his writings.

It is more than a little interesting that the Gospel of Thomas makes no reference to the resurrection even though it was written after Jesus's death and, according to Mark, Thomas was one of the eleven to which Jesus showed himself. The conclusion I draw from this is that Thomas had no illusion that Jesus was the son of Godot and in fact knew that Jesus himself did not believe in Godot as characterised by the religious texts and authorities of the time. This conflict in the legacy of Jesus is further exposed in the Gospel of John. It is obvious from this passage that there was significant disagreement about the legacy of Jesus's teachings. In John, Jesus shows himself to all the disciples except Thomas, who became known as doubting Thomas. Thomas refused to believe in the resurrection of Jesus as this would have gone against his understanding of Jesus's teachings as a wisdom teacher. John overcomes this inconvenient disagreement by Thomas by adding a significant elaboration of the resurrection tale as follows:

"Then the same day at evening, being the first day of the week, when the doors were shut where the disciples were assembled for fear of the Jews, came Jesus and stood in the midst, and saith unto them, Peace be unto you……….But Thomas, one of the twelve, called Didymus, was not with them when Jesus came. The other disciples therefore said unto him, We have seen the LORD. But he said unto them, Except I shall see in his hands the print of the nails, and put my finger into the print of the nails, and thrust my hand into his side, I will not believe. And after eight days again his disciples were within, and Thomas with them: then came Jesus, the doors being shut, and stood in the midst, and said, Peace be unto you. Then saith he to Thomas, Reach hither thy finger, and behold my hands; and reach hither thy hand, and thrust it into my side: and be not faithless, but believing. And Thomas answered and said unto him, My LORD and my God. Jesus saith unto him, Thomas, because thou hast seen me, thou hast believed: blessed are they that have not seen, and yet have believed."

John intends to send a very clear message by adding this elaboration that Thomas did eventually really believe in Jesus being the son of Godot after all. John also asserts that the faithful should not be like "doubting Thomas" and that those who believe without requiring any evidence are the ones that will be truly blessed. It is evident by the time that John was written that the resurrection was a pivotal aspect of the doctrine of the early Christian church. I am however fairly certain that, at the time of his death, Thomas was still very much doubting. I even suspect that he may have been blissfully unaware that a resurrection story associated with Jesus was even circulating if his death was prior to writing and distribution of Mark's Gospel.

It is not very surprising that Mark was influenced to add the story of the resurrection of Jesus to the end of his Gospel through, I strongly suspect, the insistence of Paul. Paul was known to be not only a Godotian, but also a Pharisee. One of the key doctrines of the Pharisees' beliefs was the resurrection of the dead. Paul was therefore likely to be absolutely convinced that Jesus would be resurrected and this was evidenced in his letters to the early church colonies.

In Thessalonians Paul is comforting the faithful, who were subject to considerable persecution at the time, of the imminent resurrection of Jesus:

"For if we believe that Jesus died and rose again, even so them also which sleep in Jesus will God bring with him. For this we say unto you by the word of the Lord, that we which are alive and remain unto the coming of the Lord shall not prevent them which are asleep. For the Lord himself shall descend from heaven with a shout, with the voice of the archangel, and with the trump of God: and the dead in Christ shall rise first: Then we which are alive and remain shall be caught up together with them in the clouds, to meet the Lord in the air: and so shall we ever be with the Lord. Therefore comfort one another with these words."

It is explicit here that Paul expects the second coming of Jesus within his lifetime and is extolling the Thessalonians to hold out until Jesus returns. With the benefit of hindsight we now know that Jesus didn't return and two thousand years later the faithful still wait in vain. As Thomas could have told them, Jesus was just a man although it would appear he was an enlightened one. Jesus was not Godot's son and he was not resurrected by Godot from the dead.

To be fair to Paul, all the initial disciples were almost certainly Godotians before meeting Jesus. As we have established in our analysis of HAB, it is very hard to break with such a powerful attachment when this has been indoctrinated into you by both your society and your religion since the day of your birth. Paul was only trying to rationalise his own beliefs with the teachings of Jesus but as we have already discussed, Jesus and Godot are entirely incompatible and the followers of the Christian Church and my poor species has suffered immensely for this ever since.

ORB:- Let me get this straight Buzzard, what you are implying is that the whole of the resurrection story arises from the influence of Paul upon Mark? Without the resurrection Jesus does not have to be divine or linked to God? What about all of Jesus's miracles?

Well again the evidence of the miracles is only really pronounced in Mark and the subsequent Gospels influenced by Mark's work. There are a few sporadic references to these in Q but these are very sparse and unsurprisingly there is no reference to miracles in Thomas, although there is some reference to healing. The references to healing in Thomas could however equally be the healing of the mind and spirit rather than the body and there is certainly no implication that any such healing is miraculous in nature. By the time of John's Gospel, Jesus is a most prodigious miracle worker because by this time, the link to Godotian belief and the further assertion that Jesus was the son of Godot were very firmly established myths. It was therefore very much in the interests, and an intrinsic part of the propaganda of the early church at this time, to build on Jesus's reputation for having miraculous powers.

ORB:- So what we have is a direct choice here, you are either in the Mark and Paul camp of committed Godotians in which case Jesus becomes the messiah and the son of God or you are in the Thomas camp where Jesus is a human wisdom teacher?

As usual you have essentially grasped the key argument. We have already explored Godot's character at some considerable length. What is the likelihood that all of a sudden he creates a human being as his son to be born on my planet and start extolling the virtues of compassion and humility? On the other hand, if Thomas is right, which is my increasingly firm conviction, then not only do many of the parables relating to Jesus's teachings in Q and Mark make sense but his teachings are also in line with other wisdom traditions. As we have said, all paths to the truth will inevitable start to converge if followed with the perspective of rational objectivity and a genuinely open mind.

ORB:- You have still not provided any evidence that Jesus in Thomas was a teacher from the wisdom tradition. Can you provide some examples and explain your reasoning?

Well this is a bit of a challenge as we have already agreed that I am not wise. The second point to make is that the sayings of Jesus in Thomas are not obvious unless the reader already has some exposure to wisdom teachings. In particular it is an important precondition to understanding Thomas to be aware of the wisdom teaching that the path to enlightenment, or becoming one with the Unot, begins with an internal journey not an external one. There are I believe a couple of reasons why the sayings in the GoT are in this secretive format. Firstly, unless someone is already on the path of self-enquiry there is little point in trying to preach to them about adopting such ideas. Their HAB will already be firmly established on the ideas indoctrinated into them from birth by the society and the associated prevailing religion into which they are born. An open mind is an essential prerequisite to the adoption of new teachings that may contradict and replace the ones previously embedded by HAB. Secondly, for a Jewish person to openly deny the existence of Godot during Jesus's time would have been extremely dangerous and the height of blasphemy. I am pretty convinced that Jesus was put to death, not because he claimed to be the son of Godot or the new Messiah, but because his teachings contradicted the established Godot based religion.

So the small challenge that you have set me is that you wish me, as a self-confessed unwise person, to interpret the words of a wisdom teacher who has masked his teachings to avoid being instantly condemned as a heretic! I shall not attempt to interpret all of the teaching of Thomas as it will take far too long and we have already acknowledged my failings but I shall have a crack at a few from my small knowledge of the wisdom traditions. The sayings are numbered in Thomas and so I shall stick with the numbering system. There are several interpretations of the exact wording of the GoT. Recognition is therefore due to the Gnostic Society Library and the translation by Stephen Patterson and Marvin Meyer http://www.gnosis.org/naghamm/gosthom.html which I have used as my source document for quoting Thomas.

3. Jesus said, "If your leaders say to you, 'Look, the (Father's) kingdom is in the sky,' then the birds of the sky will precede you. If they say to you, 'It is in the sea,' then the fish will precede you. Rather, the (Father's) kingdom is within you and it is outside you.

When you know yourselves, then you will be known, and you will understand that you are children of the living Father. But if you do not know yourselves, then you live in poverty, and you are the poverty."

This is clearly stating that the kingdom (and this is in terms of the Unot not Godot) is within each of us and is manifest in the world around us. You do not need concepts of heaven to understand "the kingdom", you just have to open your eyes and see the reality of the world around you. "The Kingdom" is not some future paradise that exists in heaven or will be created in some future time it is here and now;

51. His disciples said to him, "When will the rest for the dead take place, and when will the new world come?" He said to them, "What you are looking forward to has come, but you don't know it."

113. His disciples said to him, "When will the kingdom come?"

"It will not come by watching for it. It will not be said, 'Look, here!' or 'Look, there!' Rather, the Father's kingdom is spread out upon the earth, and people don't see it."

The GoT is also explicit that the start of this realisation is self-knowledge. This message is re-enforced by the following passages:

67. Jesus said, "Those who know all, but are lacking in themselves, are utterly lacking."

59. Jesus said, "Look to the living one as long as you live, otherwise you might die and then try to see the living one, and you will be unable to see."

This supports my notion that wisdom is a combination of information and essence. Without self-knowledge, information cannot be used wisely and will not bring about harmonious results.

The next passage refers to the knowledge that can be found by those who seek it;

2. Jesus said, "Those who seek should not stop seeking until they find. When they find, they will be disturbed. When they are disturbed, they will marvel, and will reign over all. [And after they have reigned they will rest.]"

I believe that this passage refers to the internal conflict that occurs when we realise just how constrained we are by our attachments and that this is disturbing. When they have overcome these illusions they will marvel at the reality and beauty of the world and universe surrounding them and will become one with the Unot. This will bring them equanimity and peace.

7. Jesus said, "Lucky is the lion that the human will eat, so that the lion becomes human. And foul is the human that the lion will eat, and the lion still will become human."

This passage is fascinating when we go back to our Freudian model. I believe the lion in this passage represents the unconscious attachments and instincts in the id, manifest upon the ego through the ego-ideal, and the human represents the developing independent rational ego. Freud talks about how the ego-ideal rages against the ego just as a lion rages with ferocity. If the ego matures and develops and overcomes the power of our attachments and instincts (the human consumes the lion so the lion becomes human) it is fortunate indeed for such a human. If the unconscious drivers of our psyche consume our rationality through HAB and its associated instinctive impulses and fears (the lion consumes the human and becomes human) it is very unfortunate for such a human. Such a human will attain no independent will and will be trapped in ignorance. I believe the next passage also re-enforces this point:

61. Jesus said, "Two will recline on a couch; one will die, one will live." Salome said, "Who are you mister? You have climbed onto my couch and eaten from my table as if you are from someone."

Jesus said to her, "I am the one who comes from what is whole. I was granted from the things of my Father."

"I am your disciple."

"For this reason I say, if one is whole, one will be filled with light, but if one is divided, one will be filled with darkness."

The two that recline on the couch can represent the unconscious id, and the maturing rational conscious ego. If the human consciousness can develop and escape the attachments created in the unconscious it is on the path to enlightenment and becoming one with the Unot. If the psyche remains divided the person will be trapped in the darkness of illusion and ignorance, dominated by HAB, fulfilling the needs and desires created in the id rather than the consciousness.

35. Jesus said, "One can't enter a strong person's house and take it by force without tying his hands. Then one can loot his house."

I believe that this is referring to the power of HAB, the emotions and the instincts that hold such sway on our actions and desires. You cannot overcome the power of these attachments by trying to take them on directly. Firstly the power of HAB has to be weakened through self-inquiry before the attachments and desires can be confronted and overcome. Self-inquiry is the predominant theme underpinning all wisdom traditions. The path to understanding the Unot starts within.

46. Jesus said, "From Adam to John the Baptist, among those born of women, no one is so much greater than John the Baptist that his eyes should not be averted.

But I have said that whoever among you becomes a child will recognize the (Father's) kingdom and will become greater than John."

What I believe Jesus is saying here is that no human was more committed than John the Baptist in his attempts to try to understand the nature of the Unot and commended John for not becoming distracted from this task. Despite this, even John's psyche had been preconditioned by his upbringing and the customs of the religion and society in which he was embedded. In order to really understand the Unot a mind like that of a child, looking at the world for the first time and trying to make sense of it is required. This is reiterated in this passage where Jesus says that a mature human with understanding will not hesitate to ask a child about the nature of things and become a "single one" (or one with the Unot).

4. Jesus said, "The person old in days won't hesitate to ask a little child seven days old about the place of life, and that person will live. For many of the first will be last, and will become a single one."

This theme continues:

22. Jesus saw some babies nursing. He said to his disciples, "These nursing babies are like those who enter the (Father's) kingdom."

They said to him, "Then shall we enter the (Father's) kingdom as babies?"

Jesus said to them, "When you make the two into one, and when you make the inner like the outer and the outer like the inner, and the upper like the lower, and when you make male and female into a single one, so that the male will not be male nor the female be female, when you make eyes in place of an eye, a hand in place of a hand, a foot in place of a foot, an image in place of an image, then you will enter [the kingdom]."

In this Jesus is saying that when you make the inner like the outer (development of the inner-self to enable enlightenment) you transcend identification with the body as identification with one's true being. Like a new baby with a clear mind you will then have the possibility of becoming one with the Unot, understanding the true nature of reality.

This is the hardest task for any human. In order to see reality it is first necessary to recognise and overcome the illusions that have already taken deep root in the human psyche. This is particularly difficult as society and religions, particularly God faiths, go to extraordinary lengths to indoctrinate the vulnerable human psyche at the earliest possibility. An open and clear mind is required to understand the Unot and this is the most difficult condition for any human to achieve. Many wisdom traditions make the assertion that the seeker of the Unot needs to die and be reborn in order to make real progress. This is not literally dying in a biological sense; it is the destruction of all the illusions and attachments that already populate the psyche in order to look at the world anew. This is a key theme in the GoT, Jesus states many times that the reality of the Unot (the Kingdom) is not hidden, the truth is there for those who have eyes to see. The following are some examples:

5. Jesus said, "Know what is in front of your face, and what is hidden from you will be disclosed to you. For there is nothing hidden that will not be revealed. [And there is nothing buried that will not be raised.]"

91. They said to him, "Tell us who you are so that we may believe in you." He said to them, "You examine the face of heaven and earth, but you have not come to know the one who is in your presence, and you do not know how to examine the present moment."

92. Jesus said, "Seek and you will find. In the past, however, I did not tell you the things about which you asked me then. Now I am willing to tell them, but you are not seeking them."

I think this last passage is also revealing, Jesus obviously felt that initially the disciples did not understand enough about his ideas to be able to sensibly answer their questions but later when they should have been in a position to ask intuitive questions they did not take advantage of the opportunity, they were not seeking. It is obvious from many of the passages in Thomas that both

Jesus and Thomas were exasperated by the disciples as they could not seem to grasp the message about the path to self-development and the nature of the Unot that he was trying to convey. The fact that Christianity adopted Godot after his death and the implication in John of a split between Thomas and the other disciples emphasises this point. Jesus makes a thinly veiled warning in the GoT:

40. Jesus said, "A grapevine has been planted apart from the Father. Since it is not strong, it will be pulled up by its root and will perish."

I believe this is a warning to those who were attached to the notion of a personal God faith in the form of Godot. A personalised angry God is a totally different concept from that of the Unot. This lack of identification with God also comes out in the following passage:

100. They showed Jesus a gold coin and said to him, "The Roman emperor's people demand taxes from us." He said to them, "Give the emperor what belongs to the emperor, give God what belongs to God, and give me what is mine."

Just as Jesus did not identify himself with the emperor he is equally disassociating himself from the concept of God as it was known to his audience at the time. He was also I believe, keen to disassociate himself from established contemporary teachings, many of which were ultimately included in the Old Testament, and which predicted the coming of a messiah. This prediction was patently not relevant to Jesus's teachings as he had strongly asserted that the Kingdom is already manifested in the world around them if they had but eyes to see.

52. His disciples said to him, "Twenty-four prophets have spoken in Israel, and they all spoke of you." He said to them, "You have disregarded the living one who is in your presence, and have spoken of the dead."

It is quite apparent that Jesus is exasperated by the disciples again as they are associating him with the Godotian religion of Judea at the time and once again they have completely failed to grasp what he has been trying to tell them. The disciples are saying to Jesus that the 24 prophets referred to were predicting a Messiah and that they were talking about the coming of Jesus. Jesus is quite explicit here, why listen to the predictions of the dead about a Messiah, rather they should listen to what Jesus is trying to convey about realising the reality of the world right in front of them.

Finally on the theme of attachment to material wealth and possessions there are a few pertinent quotes in the GoT which it will be well to remember when we later look at the current global obsession with extreme capitalism.

54. Jesus said, "Congratulations to the poor, for to you belongs Heaven's kingdom."

64. Jesus said, "A person was receiving guests. When he had prepared the dinner, he sent his slave to invite the guests.

The slave went to the first and said to that one, 'My master invites you.' That one said, 'Some merchants owe me money; they are coming to me tonight. I have to go and give them instructions. Please excuse me from dinner.'

The slave went to another and said to that one, 'My master has invited you.' That one said to the slave, 'I have bought a house, and I have been called away for a day. I shall have no time.'

The slave went to another and said to that one, 'My master invites you.' That one said to the slave, 'My friend is to be married, and I am to arrange the banquet. I shall not be able to come. Please excuse me from dinner.'

The slave went to another and said to that one, 'My master invites you.' That one said to the slave, 'I have bought an estate, and I am going to collect the rent. I shall not be able to come. Please excuse me.'

The slave returned and said to his master, 'Those whom you invited to dinner have asked to be excused.' The master said to his slave, 'Go out on the streets and bring back whomever you find to have dinner.'

Buyers and merchants [will] not enter the places of my Father."

The last passage from the GoT is particularly relevant. My understanding of what Jesus is saying in this short parable is that all these people were so attached to materialism that they were incapable of identifying and seeking true wealth, such as knowledge of the self and the Unot. A human dominated by their HAB has no possibility of evolving as they are utterly dominated by the greed, fear and insecurity that underpins their cravings for ever more capital as their only measure of self-worth. Seeking a meaning for one's life in the pursuit of material wealth and the all too brief associated hedonistic pleasure shows an ignorance of the human potential and is ultimately a futile existence. Even worse than just being a wasted life, this obsession with materialism and its focus on wealth extraction from society creates untold victims in the rest of society. I shall finish with the famous last quote on this theme, not from the GoT but from the Gospel of Mathew. This example is given in the context of our knowledge of Jesus from the GoT that the Kingdom of God is a realisation of the here and now not some mythical other place and certainly not Godot's kingdom.

"I tell you the truth, it is hard for a rich man to enter the kingdom of heaven. Again I tell you, it is easier for a camel to go through the eye of a needle than for a rich man to enter the kingdom of God."

We now have two scenarios; the first scenario is that Jesus was the son of Godot, placed on earth to save humankind by asking them to put all their faith in Godot through belief in him in order to go to Godot's heaven when they die. This comes with our knowledge of Godot being an angry, vengeful God that encourages genocide and tortures the souls of failing humans for an eternity. Godot inspired scenarios have been re-enacted time and time again in history by the organised religious church organisations set up in his name. This is the current version of Christianity that tries to reconcile the contradictions between the message of Jesus and the message of Godot, although, to be fair, the churches no longer explicitly sanction mass murder in Godot's name! Officers of the churches and other Godotian religions do however still bless in Godot's name soldiers from warring nations before they go into battle to kill other humans on the whims of their political masters. I think Jesus would still find this more than a little bit troubling.

The other scenario is that Jesus was a teacher in the wisdom tradition that argued that the way to salvation was through self-knowledge and escaping from the illusions and attachments that hide the truth and prevent us from evolving and realising our potential. This is an entirely consistent with the other wisdom traditions that we have discussed through the ideas of Buddhism and the wisdom revealed by the Bhagavad Gita, that so influenced Gandhi. This is the path of understanding and compassion, freedom from the entrapments of selfish desires, turning away from ignorance, attachment and anger.

I am convinced after reading the GoT that Jesus was the latter and that the early Christian church, which was after all initially created by those brought up in a Godotian faith, seriously misunderstood and subsequently misrepresented the nature of Jesus's teachings. In particular I think it was particularly disastrous that what Jesus meant by "the father's Kingdom" was equated with the Godotian concept of heaven with catastrophic consequences. The wars in the name of religion, inspired by the personality of Godot, the great God of destruction and slaughter, have raged through the centuries since this time and are the most convincing evidence that these teachings are fundamentally flawed. You really cannot have wisdom inspired wars!

ORB:- Does the GoT mention death at all? I believe that the wisdom traditions state that escaping attachment and the potential to gain enlightenment frees a human from the cycle of death and rebirth. Does the GoT state anything similar and do you have an opinion on this as this does not seem to me to be a rational proposition?

This is a difficult one for me also. Obviously humans all die, at least in the sense of the human body and, as I have previously stated, I have no evidence that satisfies my rationality that anything tangible survives bodily death. I have also stated that I have significant doubts about the concept of reincarnation but that this is not a worry as it should not influence the decisions a human makes to make the best of the life they have. The actions and state of mind required to develop and sustain an inner harmony are the same as those required to promote harmony in others and the wider world so there is no conflict here. I actually believe focusing on the issue of reincarnation and how you should behave as a consequence is itself an attachment and a distraction as you would be trying to secure some future reward. I do however recognise that I am steeped in my own attachments and as far from enlightenment as most of my fellow humans. Those steeped in the wisdom traditions with more spiritual awareness than the humble Buzzard may well be able to supply a logical argument or evidence for a tangible essence surviving mortality.

You are absolutely right to assert that the wisdom traditions do clearly state that becoming one with the Unot through the path of self-awareness does raise the possibility of transcending death. To quote the Bhagavad Gita; *"They are forever free who renounce all selfish desires and break away from the ego-cage of I, me and mine to be united with the Lord"* (the Unot). *This is the supreme state. Attain to this, and pass from death to immortality."*

Jesus does also make similar references in the GoT:

1. And he said, "Whoever discovers the interpretation of these sayings will not taste death."

18. The disciples said to Jesus, "Tell us, how will our end come?"

Jesus said, "Have you found the beginning, then, that you are looking for the end? You see, the end will be where the beginning is. Congratulations to the one who stands at the beginning: that one will know the end and will not taste death." This passage seems to repeat the theme that the mind at the beginning, before becoming ensnared in attachments and desires shares similar properties to a mind that has transcended HAB and become unified.

111. Jesus said, "The heavens and the earth will roll up in your presence, and whoever is living from the living one will not see death." Does not Jesus say, "Those who have found themselves, of them the world is not worthy"? This again emphasizes that the path to becoming at one with the Unot starts with finding the self or the spark within and transcending worldly attachments. This is completely in accord with the principles found in the Bhagavad Gita and in Buddhism.

As I have said, I cannot rationalize this very well in my own mind but I think there is one important aspect that needs to be recognized. Amongst the very strongest of attachments is the attachment to life itself and the consequential fear of death. This can cause so much anxiety and suffering to ourselves and in our actions towards others when we feel threatened. One of the most fundamental questions for understanding the true self is asking the question, "what is it in the human psyche that is afraid to die?" The Hindu sage Ramana Maharshi followed this very path when coming to his own self-realization; *"...with the death of this body am I dead? Is the body I? It is silent and inert but I feel the full force of my personality and even the voice of I within me, apart from it. So I am the Spirit transcending the body. The body dies but the spirit that transcends it cannot be touched by death, That means I am the deathless spirit."*

The closest that I can come to understanding this is that, if the instinctive attachment to life, and the part of the psyche within the person that fears dying, can be transcended, then in a way death itself has been transcended in that it is no longer a subject that troubles or occupies the mind. If at the point of death a person does not identify their self as the body that contains the self, then the end of the body is of little concern. As to what happens after the death of the body I leave this to those far more spiritually inclined than I am and, like all my fellow humans, I will eventually face this reality. What I do know is that everything in the universe is interconnected and energy transfers from one form to another so in an intrinsic sense something of what we are will always continue in some form. I think one of the most wondrous things is that all the elements that make up our bodies were forged in the hearts of dying stars. The very carbon that makes up the hydro-carbon building blocks of life were created as the result of the collapse of dying stars billions of years ago.

What I am absolutely convinced of is that neither I nor any of my fellow humans are going to end up in some Godotian hell hole being burnt for an eternity to satisfy the irrational sadism of a mythical being. This horrific vision is fortunately only the creation of my peculiar species and the ability of its highly creative imagination to build upon its worst fears. It is the very first attachment that we should all unburden ourselves from at the earliest opportunity. Carrying this burden of fear around with us only serves the purposes of those nefarious beings amongst us who exploit it as a tool of manipulation for their own purposes. The path to wisdom does not lie in fear and ignorance and attachment to such concepts. It lies in hope, understanding and a compassion for each other and the beautiful but still fragile world we share with all other beings.

I believe the similarities in concepts between the GoT, many of the parables attributed to Jesus in the Gospels in the New Testament, and other wisdom traditions are so evident that I submit that the case is overwhelming that Jesus is a much misrepresented teacher from a wisdom tradition.

ORB:- So Buzzard, if you are right about Jesus being a wisdom teacher, and from my rational perspective I am starting to find your argument persuasive, where does this leave the Christian faith now?

Well it leaves the Christian "God faith" pretty much where it is because, as we have previously asserted, Godot is irrevocably linked to Christianity. It does however offer a potential path of liberation for true Jesians should they decide to take it. The Christian church is already starting to suffer in most developed countries with year on year reductions in the numbers of worshippers attending churches. The other aspect is that in many countries, the faithful are getting older with more and more young people no longer seeing the Church relevant in their lives. I think there are two reasons for this, firstly science has advanced so far and there is so much more evidence in the archaeological record that you have to suspend all rational reason to truly believe in the Old Testament. To anyone brought up in the modern world it is obvious that it is not 6000 years old and that everyone was not wiped out in a flood 4300 years ago. The second more damning reason is that the Christian churches stand in stark contrast to all the teachings of Jesus. The Churches are dripping in wealth and populated with obvious power seeking individuals attached to the trappings of office. They are absolutely no different, in fact they are worse than the religious leaders that Jesus was so incensed about in the bible. I think that many young people cannot see how such institutions could bring them hope and enlightenment when they are so corrupted by their attachments to wealth, personal prestige, influence and the trappings of power.

Even more damning for the churches is that it has recently been discovered, particularly in the Catholic Church, that they have actively tried to conceal widespread abuse of children and other vulnerable people in their care such as the Magdalene Asylums in Ireland. The prestige and reputation of the Church is far more important to these people than continuing the work of Jesus. I have visited the museum in the Vatican, a huge edifice, which is absolutely filled with riches and possessions hoarded by the church authorities from around the world. These institutions are more like extreme capitalists than spiritual advisors. I thought it was a more than a little ironic that the Church of England were recently trying to evict anti-capitalist protestors from outside St Paul's Cathedral in London because the protest was costing them £20,000 per day in tourist revenue. Eventually even the myopic leaders in the church's hierarchy eventually stopped to reflect, albeit after the resignation of a principled officer of the church who could not stand the hypocrisy. As the public relations exercise, the image it presented was truly appalling.

The other thing is that the Christian churches largely preach the words of Godot, damning the human spirit to an eternity of suffering if they don't go to church. Followers are told to submit themselves to Godot worship and pray for forgiveness for all the sins they are supposed to have committed. Up until recently the Catholic Church even preached that un-christened babies would be condemned to purgatory. I can fully understand Godot supporting that, as the mass killing of women and children never caused any pangs of guilt or conscience, but can anyone seriously pretend that this kind of nonsense has anything to do with Jesus? This is the religion of fear and ignorance and as we know fear brings anger and shame and guilt, not the building blocks of enlightenment. Contrast the officers of the churches draped in all their finery with the simple ochre robe worn by the Buddhist priests. The Buddhists know that any fuelling of the vanities will create narcissistic attachments that will actively impede attempts at development of an objective rational consciousness.

It is my greatest desire to liberate Jesians from Christianity and the fear based Godotian heritage that goes with it. The teachings of Jesus and others in the wisdom tradition is one of hope, of the soaring of the human spirit and enlightenment, the chance to build societies that look out for the needs of the many, not the selfish aspirations of the few. Rather than worshiping Godot, it is my sincere hope that true Jesians can instead aspire to the path of self-knowledge and development and an increasing sense of harmony with the Unot.

Chapter 8 – The nature of the Unot and hope for the Jesians.

ORB:- Careful now Buzzard, you are beginning to sound a bit like a preacher yourself, maybe it's time to climb down off your pulpit for a bit! You have mentioned the Unot a lot but you haven't really explained what it is. If you are so keen to pitch this at the long suffering Jesians embedded in Christianity and to persuade them to let go of the concept of Godot, I think you need to explain what you mean by this concept of the Unot.

You are quite right; I have not really explained what I mean by the Unot. As for pitching the idea of the Unot I shall leave it to readers to make their own judgements on this discourse. As stated earlier I am very keen to differentiate between the concept of the personal Gods such as Godot who are supposed to have all the attributes of humans, only in a much greater scale and with much more scope to do havoc. The faithful who believe in such Gods genuinely believe that God will personally intervene in their lives for good or ill. This concept is so alien to the concept of the supreme overarching spirit in the wisdom traditions. Using the designation God creates the clear danger of creating a completely wrong conception because Godot is so firmly impregnated into the minds of many humans. This is why I chose the word Unot which, as we said earlier, is my abbreviation for the universal nature of things. Even more simply it is the ultimate truth, a word much used, or should I say abused, by my species, and certainly something that I believe will always remain beyond our ability to comprehend.

I have chosen the word nature because this is something that my HAB has made a strong attachment to. When I see how incredible and beautiful the planet we live on is, it often leaves me completely spellbound. Standing by the sea, seeing, smelling, hearing and even touching is almost an overload of the senses which quickly takes me away from all the petty troubles and niggles that encroach upon my mind. It never ceases to amaze me how simply incredible life on the planet is, and the extraordinary complexity of the other species that share our world. Looking beyond our planet is the vastness of the visible universe made of billions of galaxies over a distance that has to be measured in light years. We owe a huge debt of gratitude to all our scientists who continue to unravel the secrets of the world and universe around us, from the smallest particles to the largest suns.

Beyond the relationship I have through our knowledge of the universe I also have an unconscious relationship with nature that makes me want to laugh with delight or cry with compassion. Nature is indifferent to suffering; it is far beyond such human concepts. Although I have no spiritual attainment, the emotions I feel at brief fleeting moments in time when conscious of the magnificence of the natural world, and the Universe beyond, I could describe as somewhat euphoric. I am very much a being dominated by a psyche that demands to understand from a rational perspective but these fleeting moments reveal a possibility of a very different understanding which is the one revealed by Buddhist, Hindu, Jesian and other teachings. I fear that my personal limitations mean that I will never be able to join the beings who authored these texts on the path to enlightenment, but I believe that we can all benefit from their wisdom. Being at one and in harmony with greater nature is I believe a truly worthy aspiration.

All the wisdom traditions say that it is not possible to define the nature of the Unot as it is the absolute; it permeates everything and understanding would require universal knowledge. We humans only have a very small perspective on things which is actually inevitable. Let me explain this a bit more, suppose we imagine the existence of a red blood cell in our bodies. The whole existence of the cell is about 100 days. It is so tiny that the vessels that it runs through would appear so immense that they would for the most part be beyond comprehension through the sheer scale and distances involved. Each cell shares its world with 20-30 trillion others along with many other blood cells and are propelled through the body by the heart, an organ which it would have no knowledge of. It is simply being propelled by unknown forces. We as a human know we have blood and very recently in our history know that it has red blood cells in it but we have absolutely no personal comprehension of the process of creating these cells, the life of any cell or the death of a cell. Equally the cell has not the remotest comprehension of what a human is, let alone that my decision to go for a run has meant that the stream in which it lives suddenly races faster and the oxygen it contains is for reason unknown to its imagined comprehension, depleted more quickly. If it had a conscience the cell might pray to the unknown God that makes the flow, ask the God to protect it from beasts called macrophages that detect when the red blood cell is becoming frail and consumes and recycles it. Perhaps it would hope that it would be reborn? Of course we are God for the red blood cell but the sheer scale of our existence means we would have no comprehension of the prayers of the living and dying blood cells. The incredible thing is however that we could not exist as a human without the lives and action of our red blood cells and they would never exist without the imperative of our human bodies to create them. Isn't this simply magnificent?

We could look at another example; let's take a droplet of water. This is formed from vapour in the atmosphere by a cloud. The cloud and the droplet are not formed through conscious action but by the laws of nature that govern the properties of water at different temperatures and pressures. This droplet could fall onto the sea and become part of that extraordinary body of water that enables all other life to exist and scours and shapes our planet. It could fall onto rocks and emerge millions of years later. It could fall onto the poles in the form of snow and become part of a great glacier that tears the land apart as it grinds down to the sea. The water has no understanding of any of these fates or even of its own existence. Equally the sea, land or glacier would have no comprehension of the existence of the drop but without each other, none of this could take place.

In the scale and timeframe of the life of the universe the existence of our world is transitory, a blink of the eye so to speak. It would not look like a globe; it would look like a ring around the sun because in the timeframe of the universe, as opposed to man, it would be spinning so fast. The sun is at the end of an arm comprised of stars and planets spinning around the centre of the Milky Way galaxy so on this scale the earth is probably seen in the shape of a spiral. Originally our ancestors thought the world was flat and we could fall off the edge, from their perspective this is entirely logical and as previously mentioned the dear old Catholics used to burn people at the stake for denying that the sun went around the earth.

The reason for producing these examples is that there may well be some wider purpose that we play in the scheme of things. I think that the ideas of James Lovelock in Gaia theory also offer an interesting perspective about this possibility. This theory evidences the interconnectedness of the systems of the planet that genuinely appear to self-regulate to create conditions optimal for the preservation of life on the planet. We will most probably never truly comprehend what, if any, purpose we play in the larger scheme of things, because we look from the perspective of humanity in size, scope and time. This is inevitable and entirely rational and sensible from a human perspective but doesn't for one moment detract from the sheer magnificence of the universe that we are an intrinsic part of. We are very much linked into greater nature; the actions of the sun and the moon shape our environment, create the conditions for life and even affect our moods and hopes. We also have a huge impact upon our planet and upon the other beings that share it with us and with this comes great responsibility which we have largely shirked as a species.

From this I hope to give some notion of my conception of the Unot and also why the idea of a personal humanised God like Godot that we expect to hear our prayers and intervene in our lives is so incomprehensible. How could the absolute have such a relationship with us as individuals, despite the obvious attraction of this to our own vulnerabilities and the power of HAB to identify so strongly with such a concept? How would such magnificence, of almost unimaginable size, with a timescale of existence measured in the billions of years, be able to identify with the actions of my poor species? Why also would such an entity have such a needy ego as to punish us for not worshipping it enough? The impoverishment imposed by early humans of the incredible majesty of the Unot is the fact that we created Gods within the limitations of our human imagination. To be fair to the humans at the time, Godot was created when we had very little knowledge of the micro or macro universes and the forces that act within them. As Jesus in the GoT would say, the Kingdom of Heaven is both within and without us if we had but eyes to see and a mind to comprehend.

I have just argued that the ultimate purpose that life on earth and humanity fulfil in the universe may well always be beyond our comprehension in a purely rational sense. I do however feel that we can perhaps, if we can escape from impositions made upon us through the properties of HAB, be able to experience a relationship with the wider universe. It is perhaps this experiencing through the actions of the human unconscious that causes the fleeting feelings of euphoria I have previously mentioned when standing by the sea or on top of a mountain, or when new life is born onto our planet. The wisdom traditions, including Jesus explicitly in the GoT, all say that there is a spark of the divine absolute in every human life. By following the path of self-inquiry and by breaking through the illusions caused by HAB they assert that we can experience a new reality, become as one with the absolute, the Unot. I shall defer to the words of Brahman, manifest in the form of Sri Krishna in the Bhagavad Gita, *"my true being is unborn and changeless, I am the Lord who dwells in every creature."*

This then is my concept of the Unot, it is the greater nature that permeates and interconnects all things in the universe. The purpose of the Universe, if indeed there is one, is almost certainly beyond human perception, just as the purpose of the human would be beyond the perception of a red blood cell but we can experience the joy of being intrinsically part of such wonders. It also falls upon my species to have a wider responsibility, we have a responsibility to each other as we share and try to make sense of the world around us and we have a responsibility to all living creatures that share our world. At the moment, through self-interest, greed, ignorance and ambition, we run the real risk of destroying our small precious haven within the absolute. We can change the building blocks of life and harness the very power of the sun through nuclear power but we are a very long way as a species from acquiring wisdom and time is short. We have much to learn in the modern age from the wisdom of the ages that we have steadfastly ignored by living with the obvious absurdities and illusions created by the nature and origins of HAB. I would have said "by choosing to live with" but the workings of the unconscious mind upon our fragile rationality gives little scope for rational choice in such matters.

ORB:- I think I at least understand what you mean by the Unot. Perhaps it is right that it is incumbent on every human with a genuine interest in the truth

*to follow their own individual path to seek out its nature. How does this leave
the poor Christians, split between the wisdom of Jesus and the furies of Godot?*

This leaves the Christians with the same dilemma we discussed earlier. They can
continue to try to merge the incompatible and try to make sense of a religion
blending Godot and Jesus or they can liberate themselves from this conundrum.
This liberation can take the form of either turning their backs on the teachings
of Jesus (which sadly very many of them appear to already have done) and
become full blown Godotians. Alternatively they can discard Godot and adopt a
wisdom tradition based on the teachings of Jesus and the concept of trying to
understand the truth of the Unot. This will first require them to throw away the
Old Testament and much of the New Testament, such as much that is contained
in Paul's letters to the early Christian groups. It would also include firmly
disassociating themselves from Revelations which is utterly Godotian predicting
the deliberate annihilation by Godot of vast swathes of humanity. Instead they
should actively reinterpret all the limited information and attributed sayings of
Jesus in Mark's Gospel, Q, and in particular, the Gospel of Thomas from a
wisdom perspective. Rather than a religion based on fear of retribution this
process of reassessment will reveal a path to the peace, tranquillity and joy of
being one with the Unot and seeing the Unot manifest in everything around
them. Lastly and most importantly the Jesians must no longer call themselves
Christians. Along with examples of individual human compassion undertaken by
the more Jesian elements within it, this label will also associate them in the
minds of people with all the institutionalised horrors undertaken in the name of
the Christian Churches over the last 2000 years. It will also create unhelpful
associations with the existing Christian programming already firmly embedded
within their own id.

I would dearly like the followers of Godot to come clean and also refrain from
calling themselves Christians and call themselves Godotians instead, but this is
extremely unlikely. I am sure that they will continue to say as "Christians" they
act in Jesus's name whilst following Godot's will. Like the term "extraordinary
rendition", they will continue to hope that by calling themselves Christians,
nobody will actually suspect what they are actually up to! In the USA they
actually have a party called the Republicans whose leaders all claim to be firm

Christians, are dripping in wealth and whose policies are to cut taxes for the rich to feed their uncontrollable addiction to capital whilst denying even basic healthcare for the poor and vulnerable. They have also managed to create a society where over 2 ¼ million of their fellow citizens are locked up in prison whilst calling their country the land of the free. Is it just me that can see the tragic irony in this? Now I ask you, after all we have discussed about Jesus, do you really think he would want to be associated by such narcissistic self-obsessed creatures, devoid of even the slightest evidence of wisdom? I am glad he is not around anymore to see how his legacy has been so utterly abused by the manifestations of these poor creatures, who must count as being amongst the saddest examples of my poor species.

The world has never in any time in its history needed the actions of Jesians more. We have managed to bankrupt our societies both financially and morally. By moral I mean in the objective sense that our societies are increasingly unequal and out of harmony with the needs and aspirations of the majority of their people. It is the young people that I am most concerned for, they are losing all faith in the institutions of religion which, at least in the higher echelons of organised religion, seem to be run by self-serving individuals, more interested in power and prestige that delivering a coherent message of hope. The alternative to these religious models is the extreme capitalist model that worships celebrity and wealth. At the time when I am writing this, in my country alone, over a million young people are unemployed with very little hope of joining the material jamboree. Across the countries of the European Union this number is 10 million. Where is the hope and wisdom that these young people can look to for guidance and structure? When as we have discussed at such length, HAB is an intrinsic part of human nature, what is the positive model of human behaviour that they can attach to? Where are the positive examples for young people to aspire to in our societies? Many of the most deprived and vulnerable young people now display their self-worth in terms of the branding of their training shoes or the type of mobile phone they possess. It is far from surprising that many cities in my country erupted into violent riots recently; the lid of the pressure cooker of the society we have created for ourselves is fit to bust. There has never been a greater need for a coherent message of hope and wisdom.

There is, I believe, a real opportunity for a Jesian church to evolve from the current Christian churches genuinely based on the ideas of Jesus and actively committed to a search for the true reality of things. This would be a church of human development, of living life now, and most important of all, in spreading a counter culture to the extreme capitalism that pervades our contemporary society. Such a Jesian Church would renounce its trappings of wealth and its resources and structures would be placed in the service of the community or given over to charitable purposes. It would spread the message of compassion and humility and strive to create harmony in our society. It would work in the community, acting as a champion for the disenfranchised and the vulnerable and challenging those who exploit their fellow humans for their own selfish ends. There would be no finery with fancy trappings of office, gilded robes and jewel encrusted crosses, understanding that such things only promote the development of pride, power and narcissism, the properties of Godot not Jesus.

Above all, a new Jesian church would seek to develop the spark of consciousness in humanity and create a doctrine of hope and the celebration of nature and the world we live in. This church would realise that the kingdom of heaven is now but could we realise it, not in some intangible future time and place. It would embrace the magnificence of the Unot rather than the limitations of the all too human frailties and the rages of Godot. It is my species' choice whether to embrace each other and the planet we share rather than focus on selfish ends and exploitation. A Jesian church could make a very significant contribution to this end. The alternative future for the church is a long, slow and inevitable decline, fuelled by its obvious internal contradictions into virtual irrelevancy. To re-quote Jesus from the GoT, *"A grapevine has been planted apart from the Father. Since it is not strong, it will be pulled up by its root and will perish."* It is certainly taking a long time and it has resisted its demise with great determination, often through suppression, fear and acts of war, but it is slowly but steadily beginning to perish.

There are very many genuinely kind and compassionate people, dedicated to the service of others, already active in the Christian Churches but constrained by the obvious contradictions of the Godotian message and the attractions to capital, power and influence within the hierarchy. I would dearly love to set these people free to deliver a message of real hope and optimism and see the Christian temples of mammon (greed and power) come crashing down. How can you criticise greed, selfishness and avarice if you display all the trappings of these self-same attachments? Let such institutions at least be honest and categorically state that they are a Godotian cult, acting as mini Godot's on earth, demanding subjugation, homage, worship and fear of terrible retribution if not obeyed. In many ways the Godotian concept of heaven is even worse, a hedonistic paradise of self-indulgence that would bore most human beings to death (except they would be technically dead anyway) within a matter of months. Let us hope that genuine Jesians can free themselves from the clutches of the Godotians. They can then focus on trying to build a more harmonious world for my poor species, working with other learned and compassionate humans from other wisdom traditions.

Chapter 9 – The worship of mammon, the malevolent consequences on the human species of greed and avarice

ORB:- Ok Buzzard, I think you have pretty well explained the strange cults of the God faiths and the basis of wisdom thinking. I also now understand what you were saying about the self-contradictions underpinning Christianity, although I am incredulous that it has managed to survive in this form for 2000 years. Exercising my right to ask the awkward questions, I would like to steer our conversation towards the topic of extreme capitalism. What do you mean by this and why do you feel it is causing so much harm to your species?

The lust for money and possessions, or capitalism is one of the very strangest and also saddest manifestations of HAB within my poor species. It afflicts the actions and aspirations of millions and, without control, can cause the most appalling damage to societies. In most of nature, animals only exert enough effort to acquire reserves of food and shelter necessary for effective survival. Any additional effort to obtain more than this is inefficient and wasteful and nature does not usually tolerate wastefulness. In my species however the hunger for ever increasing amounts of wealth and material goods is often completely insatiable. This is now so embedded in the majority of our societies that it is no longer even questioned. We now have members of my species that have accumulated so much financial wealth that is virtually inconceivable as to how they could ever spend it. Single individuals now own more wealth than many of the poorer nations of my world. Even if they did spend it they have so many material possessions already that it is hard to conceive how they could extract even the tiniest pleasure from gaining any more.

This is such an obvious absurdity and yet these humans are actually celebrated and feted by the various media outlets as aspirational. This extreme compulsion for material wealth, through the much discussed malign qualities of HAB is very characteristic of addiction and therefore I call such humans capital addicts or capital junkies. This is a matter of considerable interest to me but before we delve into the possible reasons behind it I think it is important to highlight the degree of absurdity which is manifest through capital addiction. Going back to nature and the need to have sufficient food to survive I thought it might be useful to look at the magnitude of the current state of affairs using food as a metaphor.

Now I like food personally as my waistline often reminds me. I love well cooked meals accompanied by a good bottle of wine with coffee and chocolates to follow. I can therefore appreciate if someone is in a position to buy excellent food and drink and thoroughly enjoy the experience. If someone eats and drinks so much to be morbidly obese, no matter how fine the fare, we might start to question the sanity of this however.

Now we live in a world where food is becoming increasingly scarce and many are sadly subject to famine and starvation. Even in our so called civilised democracies, a significant percentage of the population shows signs of malnutrition because they can't afford a balanced diet and this is often represented in their life expectancy. So how would we react to an individual household that hoards vast quantities of food at the expense of the rest of humanity? If we complete the analogy with hoarding capital we can see that in the food world this would be the equivalent of also hoarding the seed that others could have grown crops with to feed themselves. Capital is the seed money of new enterprise, jobs and social institutions and should equally be invested back into the communities that have enabled it to be generated.

In my country, the United Kingdom, the wealthiest resident (i.e. benefiting from living in our society) according to Forbes in April 2011 was worth $31.1 billion. At the exchange rate of the day at $1.65 to £1.00 this equated to £18.788 billion. The average UK household had at this snapshot in history a wealth of £117,000 (this figure is a mere pipe dream to the poorest in our society). This means that the wealth ratio between our wealthiest resident and the average household in the UK is 160,581:1, a truly staggering figure.

Let us now convert this into our food category. If the average household were to empty their larders and fridges, with the food that they have at any given time to meet their consumption needs, they could probably pack this into a 1 cubic metre space.

In my country, as in much of the world, we are much captivated by a game called football in which 22 players spend vast amounts of physical effort trying to outdo each other in kicking an inflated ball between some posts at each end of a playing area. The outcome of this, as I have previously related, is a source of much passion and the different teams are very much an attraction for HAB in a surprising number of my species. The grand temple for playing football in my country is called Wembley Stadium which is so vast that 90,000 humans can sit down together and watch the object of their passion. The area of the roof of Wembley stadium (the total stadium area, not just the playing surface) is approximately 40,000 square metres. Our super glutton would fill this whole area to a depth of 4 metres for his personal consumption using our food and beverage analogy. This would be appalling enough behaviour if it was just depriving others in a situation where food, like capital, is hard to find for many people. The worst of it is that wealth is like seed, if it is distributed it can grow and create new wealth so the actual cost to society of such extremes is much higher.

ORB:- Mr Buzzard, this is simply ridiculous, we do have an understanding that you will at least try to be truthful in our dialogue. Are you seriously expecting me to believe that your species would tolerate such an obvious absurdity?

I know it is incredibly hard to countenance this with anything approaching a rational mind but in the human world very few recognise this as an absurdity. I have previously explained why it is not possible to claim knowledge of the truth but I stand by my pledge that I will only propose what I at least perceive to be true. Not only do my peculiar species tolerate such behaviour; they do, as I have previously mentioned celebrate this extreme greed and aspire to be such a person.

ORB:- But this is absurd behaviour, after all we have discussed about wisdom coming through self-awareness and the danger of HAB, why on earth would any rational human waste their life pursuing meaningless quantities of wealth?

It is my turn to reprimand you now. How many times do I have to tell you that my species is not remotely rational before the point is made? You must stop evaluating my species using a rational framework.

ORB:- Ok, I accept the chide but my part of our agreement is to try to at least approach our conversation from a rational perspective. As I am the one asking the questions I challenge you to come up with a rational hypothesis for this aberrant behaviour.

Wow, that is no small ask, creating a rational explanation for the obviously irrational. Well, our discourse is no place for the faint hearted and I accept your challenge and I shall attempt to do just that.

The accumulation of wealth has always been linked to the acquisition of power and influence in the history of my species. Those individuals who therefore achieve wealth and influence are therefore judged to have succeeded by the established principles of the majority of our societies. We can immediately see the attraction here for HAB lurking in our unconscious, if material wealth equals success and reinforces feelings of self-worth then it is an ideal object for identification within the unconscious human id. Through the id's brutal henchman, the ego-ideal, the vulnerable human ego is then put under significant pressure to demonstrate that it is managing to accumulate wealth and attract the positive attention of fellow humans. This is true of another aspect of HAB, the status of celebrity which is often seen to go hand in hand with wealth creation and also shows that the person has achieved "success" in our society. It is however the case that not all wealthy people want to attract media attention as this can also come with many awkward questions as to how wealth was actually accumulated.

If as a human being we continue to equate wealth and celebrity with success, then these will continue to be the source of strong identification within the human psyche and continue to initiate HAB. This actually links into another potential aspect of this most peculiar property of the human psyche that has been a source of continued interest for me. Why is it that when so few people actually benefit from the antics of capital addicts are they tolerated rather than reviled in society? As I shall spell out in much starker terms later in our discourse the hoarding of capital by a very small percentage of extreme capital junkies on the planet has caused very significant harm and suffering on the rest of the population. Despite this, very few humans condemn such behaviour and as stated, these strange addicted creatures are actually seen as role models. I think that the reason for this is actually on reflection quite obvious. You don't actually have to have wealth to be addicted to the concept of gaining it. Any criticism or constraints placed upon the ability of humans to collect disproportionate amounts of wealth would be seen as a threat to the object of identification already firmly established within the unconscious of many. The amount of wealth someone has accumulated makes absolutely no difference to the strength of the addiction; it is just much easier for those already wealthy to feed their further cravings. Any attempt to place limitations on the level of capital acquisition or condemning it would be received by many the same way that a heroin addict would receive news of a world ban on growing poppies.

Funnily enough, just like drug addicts I think that most capital addicts intrinsically know that their addiction is actually bad for them and doing them considerable damage. As with drug addicts, the all-consuming desire in capital addicts for the next fix is far too strong to be open to any attempts by the ego to question the rationality of further feeding the habit. It is my sincere conviction that the vast majority of the world's wealthy would actually be far happier and fulfilled as human beings if they could break their addiction and find a far more purposeful cause for the attentions of their HAB. Sadly in society, one of the other causes for attachment was supposed to be religion and this again brings us to a most interesting human absurdity. A very significant number of the world's wealthiest also firmly claim to be very religious even though every wisdom tradition strongly warns that this is incompatible with spiritual wellbeing. Jesus is absolutely explicit about this, not only in the GoT but in all the other Gospels too. Greed and the acquisition of wealth are totally incompatible to spiritual development. It is very easy to see why, firstly it creates strong attachments through HAB. Secondly it means that a person's personal wealth is more important than the needs of those less fortunate around them. This brings me back to one of my favourite groups of people with regard to making obvious points. In the United States of America, one of the most individualistic (self-obsessed) countries on the planet there is a political party called the Republicans that I have previously mentioned. All eight original candidates for the 2012 Presidential race strongly profess their belief in both Jesus and Godot and yet this party has consistently supported the needs of the wealthy over the needs of the majority of Americans. Whilst the average income of the American people has stagnated, the income of the wealthy elite has spiralled away exponentially. How did the Republicans deal with this rapidly increasing inequality? They approved tax cuts for the rich and opposed welfare reforms to provide medical support for the poor. Followers of Jesus! You just couldn't invent this stuff could you?

The people of the USA have become so addicted to capital acquisition that they now seem to equate the accumulation of material wealth and power with the accumulation of spiritual wealth. Well I think we can safely say that none of these people are from the Jesian end of Christianity. They have systematically ignored everything that Jesus had to say about the path to wisdom and the barrier presented by an attachment to mammon, so I think it's fair to say we have some true blue Godotians here.

This distorted logic, as far as I can see it, is that celebrating the ability to acquire unlimited amounts of wealth is the American way. The vast majority of Americans state that they are also "God fearing folk." Stating the strength of your faith (in Godot, of course) is also essential if you are to be considered a true American and it is currently inconceivable that a professed atheist would ever get voted into office. So if worshiping the dollar (the American currency) and worshiping Godot are both essential to the American way then Godot must approve of wealth! Can't beat the logic can you and I must express my thanks to these dear Republicans for providing such wonderful examples of the strange properties of the human psyche. This strange situation leads many poor God Fearing Americans to vote for the party that is most likely to help the capital addicts amongst them to fleece them even more, kind of sadly ironic really. Not that we should let the other side off the hook, the current Democrat President also states the importance of his Christian faith (he couldn't be elected if he didn't) but at least he has at least one eye on the most vulnerable in the society so maybe there is a little bit of a Jesian lurking somewhere inside his psyche.

I also have to be equitable on this, having been so mischievous in the use of the American examples I must not of course forget the dear old UK where I reside. The financial calamity that has overtaken my country was enabled by a so called socialist party called the Labour Party. Foremost amongst this party's policies was the stripping of regulation and oversight from the actions of the speculators in the financial markets. This enabled these speculators to not only feed the capital addiction of their clients but also gave them a virtually free hand at feeding their own capital addiction. One of the most prominent members of this "socialist" party was quoted as saying Labour was *"very comfortable with some people becoming filthy rich."* This is really just as well because the Prime Minister for most of this administration is reputed to be worth about £30 million and counting, a full blown capital addict and, yes, you guessed it, a very committed Christian! He was originally supposed to be a Church of England follower but funnily enough, the moment he left office he suddenly switched to Roman Catholicism (if I was a cynical old Buzzard, which of course I am not, I would suspect a political convenience in this sudden conversion). At least we can safely say that the Catholic Church with its vast wealth, own bank and huge temples in celebration of Godot is explicitly the most Godotian of the main Christian faiths. It does seem to be a natural home for those Godotians who also explicitly worship at the temples of Mammon. The head of this huge edifice, called the Pope, even presents himself as Godot's representative on earth which might explain the somewhat needy ego and the big hat. After all if you aspire to be the Earth's version of Godot, a bit of narcissism and megalomania will come in quite handy.

ORB:- Ok Buzzard, let me be clear about this, attachment to wealth creation and capital addiction are incompatible with following a path of wisdom and self-development. You state that this is explicit in the texts of not only wisdom traditions but even some God faiths. All the main faiths, even the Godotian based ones like Christianity state that greed and the accumulation of wealth are barriers to spiritual development and yet many prominent leaders have accumulated significant wealth, show every sign of being capital addicts yet

still profess to be devoted followers of their faith? You are right, you just couldn't invent it. Can nobody see the evident contradiction in all this?

Well this is just the thing, when even the churches seem to celebrate mammon in their actions and trappings is it any wonder there is reason for confusion amongst the masses? Don't forget, we have already raised the hypothesis that attachment to the concept of capital acquisition (capital addiction in the psyche) is very powerful even amongst many of the poorest through the properties of HAB. We can conclude from our discussions therefore that any attempt to constrain or even supplant the unconstrained capitalist model that currently blights our society will cause genuine anxiety in the psyches of many. You are threatening to take away the next fix from the junkies. This is a direct consequence of threatening the strong attachment to materialism firmly rooted in the id. With this state of affairs we have the strange situation that the capital addicts, many Religious hierarchies, the politicians and even the victims of the current model are all in some ways complicit in maintaining the status quo. I do however think that the collapse of many economies and the increasing hardship faced by many of the peoples in previously wealthy economies might be starting to put stress on this strange consensus.

ORB:- Is this addiction to capital really causing the harm that you are asserting? Maybe there is no harm in your strange species continuing in the way that they are accustomed to.

Well as you know my dear rational being, the background of our conversation was that I have this utterly unrealistic desire that my species might actually have the possibility to evolve. The future survival of our dear planet is by no means certain; the probability if we carry on in the same vein is that our actions may well prove calamitous. Do you really think the current state of affairs will meet my highly improbable aspirations for the evolution of my strangely irrational species?

ORB:- Good point well presented, Just being provocative!

To further answer your question I think it is time to look more closely at why the global financial system was virtually brought to its knees in 2008 and why without a radical change in the current human psyche this state of affairs is unlikely to be corrected.

The starting point in all this is the incredibly strong attachment to material wealth that dominates the psyches of so many of my species and their societies in the world. As previously mentioned, material success is deemed by much of society to represent success as a human and therefore by this is a natural target for HAB. It is how the majority of my species measure the value of individuals, how much they are worth. Someone who has managed to accumulate £5 million is said to be worth more than someone who has £3 million and they are not just stating this in financial terms, it has social implications too.

The strange thing is that beyond a certain point, the further acquisition of material wealth seems absolutely pointless from any rational perspective, indeed it can be considered to be actually damaging. If we look at the properties of HAB, any challenge or threat to the object of attachment by the ego is met by a series of reactionary emotions by the ego-ideal to moderate and control this behaviour. It is therefore likely for the already affluent, that it is not the further addition of material wealth that brings any real pleasure. It is the sanctions meted out by the ego-ideal on the ego as a result of any perceived failure to feed the object of id's attachment that causes distress. When someone already has many millions of pound or dollars, expensive cars, multiple houses, expensive wines in the cellar, further pursuit of material wealth and possessions seems utterly pointless. From any sense of wisdom this appears to be a pointless waste of time and energy when these people could actually be focusing on self-development. From an emotional sense however it makes perfect sense. Any failure to continue to succeed brings feelings of insecurity, emotional distress, feelings of lack of self-worth, anxiety and depression. For a multi-millionaire to actually lose some of their material wealth would feel much like bereavement in terms of the stresses set up in the psyche. These are the peculiar games played on my poor species by the properties of HAB, these people are actually quite fragile despite the fact that they are generally feted by the societies in which they are embedded.

We then have this situation that wealth is seen as evidence of being more successful that fellow humans, increasing feelings of self-worth within some humans and a source of aspiration for many others. It has therefore become a powerful source of attachment by the HAB of a great many humans. In highly individualist nations like the USA and the UK, any criticism of the ultimate correctness of the capitalistic model is virtually seen as a form of cultural heresy. The more objective truth is that this is a form of enslavement imposed by HAB that traps sad addicted individuals into a meaningless cycle of acquisition. Now although this is a sad state of affairs for those concerned it could be considered to be just another sad but tolerable example of irrational behaviour if it wasn't for the fact that the inequalities in society caused by these attachments are so pronounced. There is a very interesting book called the Spirit Level, written by Richard Wilkinson and Kate Pickett which has done extensive research into just how damaging to our societies this has become and I shall not attempt to duplicate their work in this discourse. The evidence they have produced does however seem quite compelling. This research is roundly criticised by the capital addicts who naturally rail against anything that questions what, they firmly believe, is their intrinsic right to indulge their addiction, regardless of the cost to their fellow humans.

The problem with capital addiction, as opposed to addiction to heroin, alcohol or gambling is that there is no limit to the amount that the addiction can be fed. At some point a heroin addict will overdose if they keep taking increasing quantities. Yes, there will almost certainly have been much harm caused to both the individual and the wider society, but there is a finite limit that will eventually create a ceiling for the addiction. This is similar with alcohol, at some point the abuse of the body will reach the point that the addict's body starts to fail and with a gambling addict, a point where they just cannot get hold of any more funds. With a capital addict there are very few constraints and the ones that were in place have largely been removed because of the complicit collusion of politicians, many of whom are budding or successful, capital junkies in their own right. As previously stated, we now have capital addicts in this world that have extracted more from global society to feed the cravings of their addiction than the gross domestic products of some of the world's poorer nations.

This has all come to a head because the actions of the global banking system and the simultaneous virtual collapse of any serious attempts at regulation by Governments have led to an implosion of the global financial system. No longer is it just individuals in our society that have unsustainable levels of debt but now we have whole nations teetering on the brink of financial collapse. In the UK where I live, by the end of the fiscal year 2011-12 the amount of public debt accrued will probably amount to £1.046 trillion and personal debt as of the end of 2011 at £1.451 trillion. The population of the UK stands at about 63 million so the total debt burden if you add public and private debt together averages out at about £40,000 for every man woman and child. This does not include debt accrued by businesses and financial institutions in the UK as we are not directly accountable for these as citizens. If these sums were also to be included it would probably double this figure. It will take at least a generation to recover from this dire situation. At the same time that this has been going on the capital addicts have been hoarding away $trillions in so called tax havens or secrecy jurisdictions where their vast accumulated sums are safe from Government prying eyes and the threat of taxation. As previously discussed, the damage to global finance is not just the extraction of these sums but also the opportunity costs to the society. Much additional economic activity for the benefit of all could have been generated if this wealth had been re-invested back into the societies that enabled its creation in the first place. This is another great myth surrounding capital junkies, they don't actually make much wealth for society, they just create more and more elaborate mechanisms for extracting it using the endeavours and savings of the rest of their society's members.

There was a wonderful film called "All The President's men" which looked at election scandal during Richard Nixon's presidential campaign in the USA. In this film there was a mysterious source named Deep Throat who urged the investigative reporters to "follow the money." I think this is also good advice. What has actually happened through all the complexities and machinations of the global financial system is that the comparatively few, highly successful capital junkies, often also steering the policies of global corporations, have had their addiction fuelled hunger fed by heaping debt on the peoples and nations of the world. As discussed this could almost be theoretically tolerated although it is abundantly unfair, if it wasn't also so utterly pointless.

So many of the decision making bodies in both global business and politics are now dominated by capital addicts that human societies have virtually lost control of any legitimate means for reining in these excesses. Over the last 30 years in the UK, average pay has gone up by a multiple of 3 whilst at the same time corporate pay in many of the FTSE 100 companies (Financial Times top 100 companies listed on the UK stock exchange) has gone up on average by a factor of 40 according to a recent UK High Pay Commission report. Greed is completely out of control in the UK as in many of what were previously the world's most prosperous economies. At the time of writing, a number of countries in the European Union have such high levels of debt, coupled with high levels of unemployment and stagnated economic growth that they sit on the edge of the financial abyss. This is unfortunately the consequence of the lack of any societal imposed constraints to the malevolent consequences of unrestrained HAB to material wealth. It is not just the capital junkies themselves who suffer internally from their obsessions but the rest of the global population too.

ORB:- This appears to be an even greater absurdity than some of those previously discussed. Is there no end to the consequences that HAB has for your strange species? You have people trapped to an addiction to capital who, rather than being pitied and restrained like any other addict, are actually celebrated for their malady. Is it not possible to get these people treated and restrained so they cannot do any further harm to themselves or others?

Unfortunately throughout the history of my species there have always been capital addicts, whether in the form of kings or despots or through corporate boardrooms, financiers and investment bankers. This complete absurdity as you have so rightly called it passes in the human world for normal behaviour. It is only very recently that this model is even being seriously questioned at all because it has affected the wellbeing of so many humans and threatened the collapse of nation states. The first step to overcoming this will be a developing awareness in a sufficient number of my fellow humans, that this is a problematic condition that actually needs to be addressed. This is extremely unlikely because as we have already discussed, this is a powerful attachment in the HAB of most humans, even though for the vast majority they have very little scope of feeding the cravings of their addiction.

ORB:- So is there really no hope to stop this self-inflicted harm upon your species?

We are indeed a most peculiar species, as previously mentioned. Any other species on the planet stops when they have managed to accrue enough for their actual needs, seeing any further effort as a waste of effort and energy. We must always have hope, I have said that it is very improbable that humans will be able to disengage from this unfortunate object of attraction to the properties of HAB, not that it is actually impossible. We have 3000 years of wisdom teachers attempting to offer a different path to the human species. If they didn't give up hope, often on pain of torture and death, then I don't think I should totally give up hope either.

The first hurdle to be overcome is to actually change the mind set in humans so that excessive greed is recognised as unacceptable and a sign of weakness in the psyche rather than something to be celebrated. This reminds me of what happened to the public attitude towards drinking alcohol and driving vehicles. This used to be a topic of bravado for the various drunks in the pub about how much they could consume and still drive home without actually crashing their car. Eventually however, after a long public campaign showing the damage to the lives of families of those maimed and killed by this socially irresponsible behaviour, drinking and driving has now largely become socially unacceptable. There are also strong criminal sanctions against doing this. People who drink significant quantities of alcohol and then get in their cars are now seen more as social pariahs than as good old sorts who know how to have a bit of fun.

It will take the same long hard battle to highlight the damage that capital addiction does to our societies to slowly change the public attitudes for celebrating these sad creatures to one of treating them as objects of pity and derision. This is the key to changing things. The psyche through the properties of HAB is less likely to make strong attachments to something that, rather than being a reflection of social success amongst human peers, is likely to be seen as an attachment that could lead to isolation and social exclusion. In addition, there will also have to be limits imposed by societies on the amount of hoarding and wealth extraction that any individual can get away with including associated criminal sanctions for noncompliance. The trouble is that, unlike drink driving which had very limited support in the minds of politicians; many current politicians already have strong attachments to greed and will therefore strongly oppose any attempts to seriously constrain it. There is a tremendous battle that will have to be fought in order to get acceptance in the minds of the majority that there is an acceptable social limit to the individual acquisition of resources. This is however becoming increasingly urgent in a world were all resources are finite and some are increasingly scarce.

ORB:- So how is this social limit to be defined? What is the level at which individual accumulation of resources reaches a socially unacceptable point?

An excellent question, one that I am not able to answer specifically, but it may be possible to create a theoretical model as to how the answer could be obtained. There is a concept when an organisation is looking at whether a possible project is financially viable or not, called a net present value calculation. This looks at the returns expected from an investment in a project against the rate of inflation over the time period of the project and the rate of return that this money could expect if invested in other organisational enterprises. The inflation plus the rate of return gives a figure called the cost of capital or more succinctly, the opportunity cost of doing the project. If the benefits outweigh the opportunity cost then the project is a worthwhile investment.

Any individual gathering of personal wealth has an opportunity cost to society. Could this money be better invested if it was spent somewhere else in society, re-invested into the businesses that created it or spent on socially beneficial projects for the benefits of the many. Some personal wealth accumulation is however a good thing, it enables the individual or family to look after themselves rather than looking for the state to support them. Money spent by the household is recycled through goods, services and taxation back into the wider economy creating growth and employment opportunities if the businesses that support these demands. The theoretical point for limiting further accumulation of individual wealth is the point at which the benefits linked to the individual or a family unit become outweighed by the opportunity to wider society or a business by redirecting this wealth in other ways.

There is also the question of motivation and incentives to consider. If there is no financial reward for trying to excel in work or business and adopting higher levels of responsibility then this is likely to have a significant impact on behaviour of the high number of humans who have exhibit strong HAB to material rewards. Whilst it is a legitimate question as to whether all such attachment is actually self-damaging, it is an unrealistic proposition to expect the vast majority of humans to be able to disregard these impulses and it would also require very differently structured societies. It can therefore be argued that some differentials in financial rewards linked to effort and contribution are a necessary dynamic for our societies to function. It is when these rewards become excessive and disproportionate that the social fabric of society starts to tear. Capital junkies will not accept that there is any level at which their material aspirations should be capped. In a world where there are so few checks and balances of the ability of the wealthy and powerful to feed their addiction it is necessary for society to impose a socially acceptable limit.

This then is the theoretical point at which the excesses of the capital addicts need to be controlled by wider society. It is the point when the opportunity cost to society of greed by individuals, and the organisations that act as vehicles for their indulgences, significantly exceeds the opportunity cost to society. It is not for me to determine what this figure is, this should be the role of a truly empowered democratic society. Knowing the inability of humans to regulate the appetites created by their HAB to material acquisition and resources, it is legitimate to state that it will be vital for the on-going wellbeing of any society that this figure is identified and constraints imposed. As an indulgence, I shall speculate on how such a figure could be arrived at. There are groups like the Equality Trust and others who have raised the notion that in any business or corporation, the highest paid employees should not earn more than an appropriate multiple of the average or lowest paid. Let's say that a multiple of

10 is considered appropriate. If the average employee earns £25,000 a year in total then the highest paid executive can only earn £250,000 per annum. The same could be applied to the right of an individual to accumulate capital resources. Earlier I came up with a figure in my country that the average capital acquired per capita in the UK, at the time of writing this book, is about £117,000. If we were to say that it was socially acceptable, that is the point where the social cost exceeds any reasonable personal benefit, to have a personal multiple of 15 this would enable someone to extract and hoard total material assets of £1.75 million. Any accumulated assets beyond this point would have to be reinvested back into the society that had facilitated this material gain, setting a limit on the socially acceptable level of capital extraction permitted by society. If the average wealth of a society increased then the cap on the limits for extracting wealth could also theoretically increase in direct proportion.

If we were to combine these two models we would then have a situation within any given society and business within it that nobody in a business could earn more than 10 times as much as the average salary in that business and no individual could extract more than 15 times the average wealth accumulated in any given society. This allows plenty of scope for aspiration and differentiation to be aspired to and to be valued by most humans, without enabling obscene levels of inequality to exist with all the individual and societal consequences that come with this. As stated, these are just figures I have come up with to make the point, it would be up to due process and I am sure considerable academic argument in any given society to determine what these figures should actually be.

ORB:- This seems an eminently reasonable and sensible proposition for limiting the excesses caused by capital addiction. It enables some in society to be motivated and rewarded for their endeavours without this becoming excessively damaging and exploitative. Why hasn't something like this been simply adopted?

You have absolutely no comprehension as to the howls of outrage that would be heard by most humans if you attempted to put a limit to the magnitude of the resources they aspire to acquire. We have already discussed that beyond a certain point it becomes utterly pointless or even damaging for humans to continue to feed the addiction to greed arising from the perverse properties of their HAB. All the wisdom traditions give strong warnings as to the incompatibility of attachment to material reward. It is seen as an impenetrable barrier to developing the self-awareness necessary to follow the path of understanding and harmony with the Unot. In fact, the very nature of self-awareness would rapidly reveal the pointless futility of chasing ever larger pots of gold at the ends of an endless series of rainbows that always rapidly fade away to nothing. As soon as one material object is achieved it immediately loses its golden lustre and the mind is immediately sent off to hunt for the next object of desire to meet the insatiable cravings initiated by HAB in the psyche.

We have also introduced the concept that it is highly damaging to society if capital addicts are allowed to feed their obsession beyond a certain level. This was spectacularly manifested in the recent collapse of the global financial markets (which was really not very wise was it?) and the associated huge debt obligations of both the majority of individuals and nation states. No matter how strongly and rationally these arguments are made they are likely to come to nothing. There are very few drug addicts that will be prepared to curtail their addiction to drugs just because it is both damaging to themselves as individuals and to the wider society they live in. Exactly the same applies to capital addicts, the only way that their behaviour would voluntarily change is if their unconscious was to make an even stronger attachment to something other than capital to identify with and aspire to.

There are formidable barriers to changing the current obsessions with celebrity and wealth. Not only are the reins of power mostly in the hands of fully fledged or yet aspiring capital addicts, but the barriers to entry of others are deliberately considerable. If we just look at my own country, the Labour party has huge debts and only managed to finance the last election campaign through the direct contributions of the trade unions who have their own very specific vested interests. Much of the Conservative party campaign was financed by a billionaire arch capitalist with opaque finances hidden away in a multitude of complex corporate vehicles in various secrecy jurisdictions. Despite the fact that only 7% of the UK population actually go to fee paying private schools (bizarrely known as public schools) over 50% of the current Government cabinet come from such privileged backgrounds. In addition, much of the media that shapes public opinion, particularly relevant during election campaigning, is also firmly in the hands of a few capital addicts who use their media outlets to peddle the privilege and merits of the capitalist agenda.

In the current system, the only methodology to finance an electoral campaign is through financing acquired from those who will very much call in their favours and influence the formation of policy after the election. In the USA it is far, far worse, the election campaigns run for pretty much 12 months every 4 years, not counting the intense lobbying and manoeuvring that goes on in between. Enormous sums of money are required to fund these campaigns and this makes the succeeding candidates very much indebted to those that financed their path to office. Through these mechanisms the interests of the capital junkies are sustained regardless of the administrations that are voted into office by an increasingly disillusioned and disenfranchised public. Reining in excess in such circumstances is like trying to convince a bunch of drug addicts to stem the ability of society to fuel drug addiction, whilst putting the same addicts in charge of the drug procurement policy for the National Health Service.

ORB:- I thought the prevailing type of Government for many of your species was called democracy which, unless I am very much mistaken, means "rule of the people", yet the scenario that you have portrayed reveals virtual exclusion of the people and rule by vested interest. Again your peculiar species seems to be using one word to describe a system that appears to be utterly contradicted by reality and again I find myself rather confused. How did this strange turn of events occur?

I shall explore a bit of the history and speculate as to the cause of this. The main mystery to me is however the fact that a system which preserves the interests of a minority of capital addicts and promotes ever increasing levels of inequality is actually tolerated by the majority of people. First a bit of history, democracy is a word that is most associated with ancient Greece from about the 7th century BCE. Despite this ancient origin of the concept, modern democracy is a comparatively recent event and the concept of one person, one vote even more recent. It was only in 1928 that women got the right to vote on equal terms with men in the UK (probably as a consequence of the old patriarchal Godotian based religions that have overtly influenced thinking for two millennia). For virtually the whole of the recorded history of my species, the majority of people had very little influence whatsoever over whom their political masters would be. Even in countries where there has been fledgling democracy, this has often been interrupted through the intervention of vested interests in the military or by the rise and fall of dictatorships. The current situation where we have a preponderance of the wealthy and privileged, dominating the positions of power in our democracies and convinced of their sense of entitlement is actually a familiar model of government for our species. I think it is this historical familiarity, coupled with self-identification with figures of authority in the unconscious id, that has enabled the successful subjugation of the majority by a self-interested minority.

The remarkable thing is that the exploited majority are rather like animals who believe they are trapped in a cage whilst the cage door is actually open. They rail against their inability to change the nature of their lives when they actually have the key to their own emancipation readily available through the democratic process. They are simply too conditioned or apathetic to realise it. It will require quite a phenomenal change in the collective psyche, to challenge the sense of entitlement for those who gorge on society's resources. In all probability they will continue to feed their greedy obsession with complete disregard for the consequential damage inflicted upon their fellow humans.

The capital junkies will naturally insist that their voracious appetite is actually a benefit to society and that they should continue to be feted and celebrated. One of the most interesting apparent myths is the one regarding how clever the brokers and traders in the investment banks actually are and how this incredible skill justifies astronomical salaries and bonuses. An interesting insight into this was revealed in an article on a book called "Thinking Fast and Thinking Slow" by Daniel Kahneman, published in a newspaper called the Observer here in the UK. In this article vast numbers of the transactions undertaken by traders were analysed against what would have happened if the traders had just left the money alone in the existing stocks and sat on their hands.

The result was quite extraordinary; the correlation between the traders' activities and wealth creation was absolutely zero. The evidence presented suggested that at any one time, 2 out of 3 of the funds being managed by the financial institutions actually underperform the market, and let's face it, the market has been pretty poor for a long time now. Each of these financial transactions carries a management charge, used to pay for the huge salaries and bonuses that predominate remuneration in these institutions. Lord Turner of the Financial Services Authority once famously stated that the City had grown far too big and much of its activities were "socially useless" (but obviously not if you are a Capital Addict and the purpose is to feed your addiction). Here's the revelation: not only were the City's financial institutions extracting vast sums of money from society being socially useless, but the evidence would suggest that they appear to be financially useless to the majority of society as well. The return on most investments by the majority of the population that have pension plans and other long term financial instruments is truly miserable. This is condemning millions to a life of relative poverty in their old age whilst the financiers responsible for this debacle pay themselves ever increasing returns.

We earlier looked at the increase in salary between average UK workers, which went up by a factor of 3 over the last 30 years and many of the executives from the FTSE 100 companies that went up by a factor of 40 during this time. Naturally we should then expect to see the FTSE 100 index increase by a similar amount, a factor of 40, to justify the disproportionate rewards being channelled to these high priests of mammon. 28 years ago in April 1984 when the index was started it stood at 1138.3 and in February 2012 as I write this it stands at 5899 which is a far less than staggering 5 times greater than approximately 30 years ago. This means that the top executives have rewarded themselves at 8 times the rate that they could reasonably have justified owing to the increase in the stock values of their companies. There is absolutely no equivalence in the rate of, largely self-awarded, rewards paid to these people and any sensible measure of performance. This is just one piece of a large body of evidence that strongly indicates that, rather than creating wealth for our society, the current global financial system and the addicts that feed from it represent a large malevolent vehicle for extracting wealth from the large majority to feed the appetites of a sad but greedy small minority. This is, as we have stated, unlikely to change whilst those who profit by association with this dynamic, are overly represented in the ranks of our politicians, ensuring that this system is largely protected from interference by the disenfranchised majority.

This is all so predictable if we go back to our basic model of the human psyche and the properties of HAB. If you appoint capital addicts to the boards of corporations and financial institutions they are going to run these to feed their personal addiction. They are certainly not going to run them for the best interests of shareholders who get the scraps from the tables after much of the profits have been extracted, and they are definitely not going to run them in the interests of society as a whole. It is not even that this is a deliberate policy made by many of these people; we must never forget that these attachments are made in the unconscious and their actions are therefore pretty much a mechanical response by their egos responding to these powerful demands. If their egos had actually matured and acquired wisdom they would not be wasting their lives extracting and hoarding resources. Instead they would be involved in harmonising their psyches for their own internal benefit. This would have a resulting impact upon their external actions which would also become engaged constructively in creating a harmonised society for the benefit of their fellow humans.

I am sure that many genuinely believe that in some strange way their insatiable desire to secure entirely disproportionate resources is somehow benefiting wider society rather than, as all the evidence suggests, actively harming it. There is this theory, much favoured by the insatiably greedy called "trickle down." In this theory the vast sums hoarded by the capital addicts somehow finds their way back into society. Some of it does, but a much larger percentage is effectively extracted, inhibiting wider investment and growth in society. These sad humans are as much victims of their own natures as the rest of humanity. There are remarkably few people who, having come to the realisation that their life is pointless and harmful would continue to act in the same way. Their ids and ego-ideals will continue to do everything in their power to prevent the ego straying from the object of their attachment. This realisation is therefore mercifully, for their personal sense of self-worth, extremely unlikely to occur.

This brings us back to an earlier point, as capital addicts not only will not, but actually cannot, rein in their hoarding inclinations, it will require society to forcible act to constrain them. This will require the levers of power to be firmly removed from their grasp and placed into a form of government that genuinely seeks to meet the desires and aspirations of the majority. This would require the creation of a new political consensus to create societies with a focus on collective responsibility rather than self-interest. This is extremely improbable.

ORB:- what would such a society look like? How would it differ from what you have now?

This is an extraordinarily difficult question to answer and it is rather daunting to even attempt to do so. I believe it should really be down to the young humans, having to deal with the consequences of the appalling mess that my generation has made for them, to decide how future society should look. However perhaps it is possible to bring together a few guiding points that would certainly help to create a more harmonious society. Before I do this I think there is a far more important question that has to be answered. If having a life simply hoarding ever increasing amounts of resources is utterly pointless and damaging to others, and submitting yourself to a mythical narcissistic angry God appears less than wise for your inner harmony, what alternatives are there? In effect ORB, this is the big one, what other purposes could create meaningful but positive attachments? If we can't answer this question for ourselves how can we expect to create a society that serves these aspirations.

ORB: Isn't this what the wisdom traditions tried to communicate, the path of self-enquiry leading to understanding and increasing harmony based on an increasing understanding of the nature of the Unot?

Indeed it is which begs the question, why have the aspirations of the wisdom tradition failed to create a wise and harmonious world? Is it really realistic to expect a species that is dominated by the powers of HAB to universally be able to follow the path laid down by the wisdom traditions to create an enlightened society? I think this would be a more realistic prospect for a species like yours ORB, not mine. Following the path of the wisdom tradition is therefore very much a personal journey but is unlikely to be a path followed by the mass of humanity and there are sound reasons for this. Introspection is always a good place to start so I shall just spend a bit of time looking at my own attachments which I, like I am sure most of my fellow humans, would be quite reluctant to give up. Firstly I have a wonderful relationship with a lady who has been my partner or, as I prefer to say, soul mate for over 20 years. We have a full understanding that this attachment will cause one of us a great deal of personal suffering when one of us dies, except in the unlikely event that this happens simultaneously. Having full knowledge of this fact and the emotional turmoil that is the inevitable result does not for one second make me question the wisdom of this attachment. I have absolutely no desire to change it.

This is where I shall do my quick bit on the powerful positive attachment to another human more commonly referred to as love (a word with as many connotations as the word God). This can be a wonderful thing or quite a sinister thing depending on the attitude of the other person. Here the wisdom tradition gives a very useful perspective. If your actions towards this person are towards helping them to achieve harmony within and achieve their positive goals in life, provided of course that this is not at the expense of causing harm to another, then this is a positive indicator for a happy successful relationship. Such love can unfortunately sometimes lead to separation and emotional heartache if the life goals of the two persons draw them away, but unselfish love would accept this as a necessary price. Love can however also be possessive, an identification made within the unconscious that creates insecurity and objectification. This type of attachment can create controlling behaviour and actually damage the object of your affection. Possessive attachment is usually highly destructive in the long term for the parties involved as insecurity creates anger and intolerance and an attempt to control the behaviour of the partner for selfish desire. This type of love can only lead to disharmony.

Back to my attachments, I am very partial to red wine and enjoy my food far more than is probably healthy and, as my waistline attests, certainly more than is necessary for survival. I have a motorbike which I ride around on when the weather is nice (yes I am a fair weather biker in answer to true devotees) and makes me imagine that I am some kind of free spirit. I also like loud music, probably from my adolescent affinity to punk rock music. All these things bring a colour and hedonistic pleasure to my life that I do not want to give up, even although I am sure that none of them are remotely helpful to following a spiritual path. I am therefore the last person in the world who should be preaching to my fellow humans that they should give up all the attachments that their HAB is automatically creating for them. In summary, if the path of ruthless self-enquiry is not the path for me, even though I can see that this should really be the ultimate goal for any human, then I cannot realistically expect this of others.

We can however indulge our attachments through a wisdom lens. If the actions arising from our attachments are not doing any significant harm to either us, or more importantly for any responsible human, harm to anyone else, then I think the world can accommodate these things. Again, the real test for this is whether the actions arising from these attachments are likely to promote harmony within and without or at least, not cause any significant disharmony? Often, just like attachment to resources and material wealth, the answer to this may lie in moderation rather than excess. As I have mentioned, I like a nice glass of red wine, but drinking this to excess will damage my health, damage my finances, probably make me anti-social to others should I become drunk, and cause significant risk of harm should I be irresponsible enough to try and drive. In moderation however it can bring me a pleasant contentment, can fool me into thinking I am convivial company, and will help create a livelihood for the growers of grapes and the producers of the wine. The same can be said of my love of food or even my dear old motorbike, provided I ride this responsibly, although I recognise that burning up fossil fuels for hedonistic pleasure may not ultimately pass the harm test!

Chapter 10 – speculation on the structure and nature of a wise society

ORB:- *So what you are saying here is that it is unrealistic to expect the majority of your species to be able to overcome the power of HAB, but that some of the resulting attachments are better than others and the harmony test is a good measure of this? Is it therefore possible for you to conceive of a society, that accommodates human nature, but mitigates the harm that can be caused when HAB is unconstrained, or when the objects of HAB are actually harmful and damaging?*

Exactly so. There is no point in trying to create a perfect utopia that is completely incompatible with HAB, this would require many generations of evolution although it is perhaps a desirable ultimate destination and liberation that I could perhaps wish for my species. It is also unrealistic to expect us all to create mature egos through rigorous self-enquiry from the underdeveloped and needy egos that predominate in my species as exhibited by myself. It is however perfectly appropriate to enquire as to how HAB can be accommodated responsibly. This will require a society to be developed with appropriate checks and balances to rein in inappropriate attachments and harmful actions resulting from HAB. This will still be a very different looking society to the one that we have now and it will be extremely difficult, but perhaps not entirely impossible, to develop. This slim possibility will rely on whether enough of my fellow beings are sufficiently alienated and unhappy with the existing state of things to make a concerted effort to change them.

It is a strange aspect of HAB in my species that this can manifest itself in the most inconceivable cruelty and senseless mutual slaughter of others and equally can produce extraordinary acts of self-sacrifice and kindness. The strangest thing about this dichotomy is that these events could manifest from the same person depending on what is being stimulated in the unconscious and the environment in which they find themselves. We have already talked about the strange happenings in Germany from early in the 1930's until the end of the global war in 1945. The German people were not intrinsically cruel and callous but they were an intrinsic part of a state that caused the death of tens of millions of fellow humans. I firmly believed that their collective psyches were eroded through a combination of fear and identification with some very nefarious but charismatic human figures through the properties of the human ego-ideal. This is an extreme example of how the peculiar properties of the HAB, working within a population that has a shared identification with a set of powerful ideas, can cause havoc to my species. Those who did not identify with these ideas would have been manipulated into compliance through fear and peer pressure. It takes great bravery and a highly evolved consciousness to stand up against such a dynamic.

Equally, I have seen examples of extraordinary kindness and self-sacrifice by people. One of the ones that gives me a great deal of joy and I always use as example of the best of Britishness is the London Marathon. At this event over 30,000 competitors and millions of sponsors participate in an event that not only allows the runners to meet personal goals and achievements, but also raises millions of pounds for charities. Many of these charities support the most vulnerable in our communities or aim to protect other species from the harm that humans can cause. I also remember with great emotion the Live Aid concerts to help the victims of famine in Africa back in 1985. There was such positive emotion at the time that I, like I am sure many other young people on that night, felt that my life had a very different purpose and meaning, rather than just focusing on my own selfish needs. There are so many fellow humans who continue to dedicate their lives to helping others, often with considerable self-sacrifice. Sure you could say that this is also selfish as it can create feelings of purposefulness and self-worth which are properties of HAB but this is HAB working with the intention of delivering compassion and creating harmony rather than selfishness and division.

The point I am trying to make here is that, if you cannot hope or even desire to remove the properties of HAB from the human psyche, you can strive in the attempt to construct a better society to create positive objects of attachment and purpose rather than destructive or selfish ones. The unconscious will make its attachments anyway as this is a basic human function but there is much more hope for a positive outcome if there are positive objects of attachments and a culture of mutual responsibility is established, rather than celebrating selfishness and avarice.

Unfortunately in countries like my own, the UK, we have built a society that celebrates self-interest and greed and this is replicated to a greater and lesser extent throughout much of the human world. I call this viral capitalism as, just like a biological virus, this mind-set infects and pollutes the societies that are exposed to it. A wise society, mirroring how a maturing ego frees itself from unconscious instincts and attachments through rigorous self-enquiry, will free itself from the more malevolent consequences of HAB through imposing controls upon the collective psyche of the population. In a democratic society this, quite rightly, requires consensus, but we are now fully conditioned in our addiction to greed and are unlikely to submit willingly to rational constraint.

This is a fundamental flaw with the democratic process through which politicians get elected by promising what is popular and then doing largely whatever they want after they have got into power. A classic example of this, and one worth exploring is here in the UK. The present Prime Minister (2012) from the Conservative Party, is a fully-fledged capital addict with a sizable and growing personal fortune although he is quite naturally elusive should you try to pin him down on this point. He realised that he would never get elected into power unless the electorate trusted him with one of their most cherished national institutions, the National Health Service. Quite rightly when you have a predominance of financial self-interest underpinning a party's culture the UK electorate were highly sceptical of the Conservative health agenda. The Conservatives as indeed did "New Labour" under their arch capital addict leader, have had a habit of hiving off public assets by passing them into the hands of private corporations. The historical reality of this with our train services, energy companies, water companies etc. is that almost universally the consumer ends up paying inflation plus price rises for a derisory quality of service along with spectacular rises in boardroom pay. In the majority of enterprises operating in a truly competitive open market, prices in real terms for products are constrained and efficiency improvements are essential for business survival. In these enterprises however the market is far from efficient, competitive or open and therefore there little evidence of such behaviour. One good reason why the standard of living is crumbling away in the UK for the vast majority is this inexorable rise in the cost of services and utilities. Why then would anyone trust the Conservatives with the NHS?

To avoid this healthy cynicism the Conservative Party made a pledge to the electorate before the last election that there would be no large top down (for which we can say Government organised) reorganisation of the NHS under his stewardship. He had absolutely no intention of keeping his word! The Conservatives scraped into office with the help of a coalition with the Liberal Democrats. No sooner had he crossed the threshold of number 10 Downing Street (the Prime Minister's residence) than the Conservatives announced their proposal for the biggest re-organisation of the National Health Service since its creation. At the heart of this proposal was a privatisation agenda which will of course, based on overwhelming historical evidence already discussed, make very nice profits for budding capital junkies in the boardrooms of the suppliers at great cost to consumers.

Now the arch masters of making profit through healthcare privatisation are the Americans. The average person in the USA pays 2 ½ times as much for their healthcare (OECD figures) as we do in the UK. So this begs the question as to why any conscientious cost aware UK Government move towards a profit based system, which will almost certainly cost much more to deliver and runs huge risks for service provision? Even more importantly for our wisdom agenda, in the US a large segment of the population is effectively excluded from effective healthcare under their profit based system. Humans are allowed to die in their droves whilst the profits for the greedy continue to grow. Capital addicts as we have discussed, will be primarily concerned with building their personal and corporate capital hoards rather than the wellbeing of patients (who become just a mechanism for capital extraction).

So why on earth is the Government so set on taking this extremely perilous and risky path? Well rather unsurprisingly one of their number, now a somewhat discredited individual through questionable associations, who held the Shadow Health Portfolio between 1999 and 2003, had links with a so called charity called Atlantic Bridge. This linked top Tories and right wing Republican (yes we are back to my favourite band of capitalist, Godotian inspired Christians) activists. Officially this was a charity but in fact, it was a meeting place for the movers and shakers of the right wing. Some of the most influential architects of current (2012) Government policy were all on the Atlantic Bridge advisory council. Even more interesting was that its sole employee was apparently paid for by £25,000 pounds from the US drugs giant Pfizer. Now what motivation would a US drugs giant have for so openly involving itself in the affairs of Atlantic Bridge? Are we really supposed to see this as an act of philanthropy or can we draw our own, far more concerning conclusions that they were there to lobby the politicians whose decisions could further their interests. So here we have many crucial founders of current UK Government policy, linked to an organisation with explicit connections to US health giants and free health market lobbyists. Are we seriously expected to believe that all these lobbyists have not had any significant impact upon future Government thinking on health?

Important recap – the USA system excludes large elements of its population and cost 2 ½ times as much per capita to supply healthcare (OECD figures) as the existing National Health Service. The acolytes of this appallingly flawed system, making huge corporate and personal profits, were directly influencing future UK Government thinking on healthcare! It is no surprise then as stated that the leader of the Conservative Party, after making copious speeches in the election of no more radical top down reorganisation of the NHS, immediately launched his radical reorganisation of the NHS with privatisation at its core upon election as Prime Minister. Many of the same corporate giants that squeeze the lifeblood out of the US system will now be given every opportunity to do the same to the UK health service, at huge cost to both services and patients.

ORB:- Buzzard, you are losing me here, this is all very interesting I am sure and no doubt of great concern to the people of the UK but how is this related to our discussion for the potential development of wise societies?

I have gone into this to highlight the extraordinary extent that vested interests have permeated every element in our so call democracies, and also to illustrate the mendacious lengths that politicians will go to in order to get elected. The important thing from a wisdom perspective is that free healthcare to everyone in society; regardless of their ability to pay, is an extraordinarily important and positive force for building a harmonious society. The most bizarre claim that the Conservatives have come up with for their agenda is that we cannot as a country afford to support the NHS in its current form. This is when we already know that the US model costs 2 ½ times as much per person as ours does in the UK. What they really mean is that the capital addicts in our society are not prepared to subsidise the welfare of the less fortunate by subsidising the costs of the NHS, but they are quite prepared to pay a fortune in private healthcare provision to look after their own selfish interests. Their HAB induced desire to grow their personal capital hoards and extend privilege to themselves, even if it ultimately costs them more in real terms, overrides any sense of wider responsibility. What we have here is the classic conundrum that despite having a parliamentary democracy, the majority, who will be entirely disadvantaged as a result, have elected a political party who deliberately misled them about their intentions and who explicitly serve the interests of the greedy. Do you now see why I have gone to such lengths over this example? It effectively shows the incredible difficulties that will have to be overcome in order to create societies inspired by wisdom instead of HAB inspired avarice.

Politicians fully understand how to manipulate the weaknesses in voters in order to get elected, particularly by deliberately getting people to focus on self, rather than collective interest. Politicians know that creating a fairer and wiser society does not readily appeal to selfishness within people so they usually promise to cut taxes or spend more on popular programmes, without the finances to do this. This is the cause of much of the debt in the previously developed economies after national politicians spent large sums of money they didn't have, to finance popular public spending or tax cuts in order to get elected. This was enabled through borrowing from the speculators in the capital markets who as we know extracted vast amounts of wealth from the system. We know through analysis of the outcome of all this that the resulting debt burden ended up on the laps of the majority and particularly upon the most disadvantaged and marginalised in society. Effective politicians create false but alluring pictures in the minds of the electorate that inevitably become objects of attachment if seductive enough. People will readily vote for politicians that effectively implant these, often deliberately false pictures. In reality both the politicians and much of the electorate instinctively know that these are false images, but they are often so much more attractive to the human psyche than facing up to stark realities.

ORB:- This truly is a bleak assessment, once again you lead me to the verge of despair of any rational future for your species.

Well let's consider this despair liberating. As the task appears virtually hopeless (but as you know I never entirely give up on my irrational attachment to hope) then we have absolutely nothing to lose by discussing some of the other hurdles that will have to be overcome. As stated, I think it is for the young to decide the shape of future society but as this is our conversation there is nothing to stop us from further speculating and exploring some ideas.

ORB:- Speculate away Buzzard

We have looked at HAB to God faiths and to greed and have found both of these wanting from a wisdom perspective. This basically eliminates the most prevalent attachments for the majority of my species. This is all well and good but when we have a species that is programmed for attachment this leaves an empty void, a wandering psyche that has no point of reference to latch onto. Now this is all very well for those who are set upon the journey of self-realisation but as we have said, this is an unrealistic path for the majority who would be in serious danger of being cast adrift. The various servile followers of mythical Gods like Godot are extremely unlikely to wish to escape from their attachments and this also applies to the capital addicts. Both of these models, one based on fear and insecurity in the unconscious, and the other naked self-interest, are far too alluring. We are however speculating so what alternatives could we provide?

We have already described the incredible and spectacular nature of the Unot and at least for myself, one of the most rewarding attachments is to realise that we are all an integral part of this. As the most prevalent and empowered species on the planet we should take great joy in this relationship but also gracefully accept that it also comes with great responsibility. We are the custodians of our beautiful world but we are damaging its beauty and threatening the wellbeing of all the other creatures that share it. The first wise attachment that I would promote is therefore to attach ourselves to the idea that we are the custodians of this world and should dedicate ourselves to its preservation on behalf of all the species that inhabit it and for future generations of our own. Certainly if we can combine this with humility, self-reflection and realisation it would very much add to our inner harmony but even a positive attachment to such an idea is a good start.

As in the God faiths, I actually believe that the root cause of attachment to greed and self-interest is also based on feelings of fear and insecurity in the human id. There is no rational reason for this hunger to accumulate regardless of actual need but it makes a perverse kind of sense if this is linked to a more intense vulnerability in the human unconscious. Material resources cannot ever alleviate this insecurity but the process of acquisition at least distracts the psyche from dwelling upon it. We can however as a species offer a far more powerful alternative. What if we were to find security in our relationships and the responsibility we accept for the wellbeing of each other? This could actually stimulate the dynamic that could lead to harmony.

Time here I think for a little metaphor and this time we are off to ancient Greece for its source. In the time of ancient Greece there were fearsome soldiers called Hoplites who had a large round shield and a spear or sword. Hoplites were formidable in themselves but far more fearsome and effective when working as a group known as a phalanx. The effectiveness of the phalanx actually depended on mutual trust between the Hoplites because of the nature of the close up intensive fighting of the time. When thrusting with the weapon in the right hand the Hoplite was exposed to attack by the enemy. He could however be protected from this attack by the shield of his comrade in arms to the left. The very survival of each Hoplite in battle and any chance of victory rested in the complete trust in the capability and training of his comrades. Any Hoplite who was selfish, lacking in trust and only looking out for their own interests was not only ultimately more vulnerable, but also would cause great distress to the whole Phalanx and ultimately jeopardise the whole interests of the army and the home community it served. We have built modern societies largely comprised of selfish Hoplites. Yes for our modern Phalanxes (representing the structures of our societies) to work we will need to sacrifice some of our independence of action and particularly our greed but the rewards could be astounding. What I am therefore proposing here is the understanding that real security would rely on the actions that we undertake for the benefit of others, having trust that this will be largely reciprocated. This is a worthy target for our HAB, it would eventually lead to social reproach and sanction for those who deliberately broke their trust and responsibilities to others. At the moment in our greed celebrating societies, acting with self-interest, often knowingly to the detriment of others, is the celebrated norm not an aberrant exception.

Let's follow this logic using the example of the National Health Service in the UK as our "Phalanx." If it was unacceptable for anyone in our society to pay for private healthcare and all provision had to be accessed through the National Health Service it would create an extraordinary change in the dynamics of the behaviour of both the politicians and the capital addicts in our midst. All of a sudden we would suddenly find our highly cost effective solution to health was not only deemed to be affordable but you could guarantee a virtual insistence from the most fortunate in our society to want to invest more in it, not less. When the personal wellbeing of the wealthy is intrinsically tied into the wellbeing of the poor and vulnerable it will create a wonderfully positive and harmonious dynamic.

The capital addicts in our midst would rage against the breach of their basic right to "feather their nests" at the expense of others in society but is this really the sort of society that we want to live in? I am absolutely convinced that Jesus (the wisdom version) would absolutely love this model. At the moment we have many of his so called followers more than happy to watch their fellow humans die so that they can invest their personal wealth for their own selfish ends rather than to the benefit of all. Yes I know that the likelihood of such a radical change in human behaviour is remote but in theory at least it is entirely possible and society would be so much better as a consequence. The interesting thing is that eventually, even the wealthy would be happier in this model as the quality of provision was raised for all. Remember, in the USA it costs 2 ½ times as much per person and even the wealthy can be left in dire need if they have a "previous condition" that means exclusion of treatment or exorbitantly expensive health insurance premiums. If I was them I would vote for the Phalanx solution rather than the wandering Hoplite every time!

The same logic applies to other essential services required for an effective society. In the education system the wealthy and even those who aspire to be, will pay significant sums of money to put their children into private education. Just as with health, if everyone had to get their education through state funded schools, the privileged in society would spend a lot more attention to the quality of local provision and many more resources would be channelled to enhance the quality of education provided. The hypocrisy of some politicians in my country, who are after all responsible for enhancing the quality of education, has been astounding. Even some of those who are supposed to be socialist in inclination and purport to stand against privilege through wealth, channel their own children to private schools as they don't have confidence in the quality of state provision. Just as in the NHS, if everyone in the country had to turn to state provided education, quality would rapidly rise for the benefit of the many. In the current model, the greedy cream off much of the best educational provision for the benefit of their own self-interest.

The first obstacle to overcome in order to change the current structure of society to a wisdom model is the nature of the current democratic process and our model of parliamentary democracy. We have discussed how the cost of financing political parties and the election campaigns creates a process of continued indebtedness in politicians to those who choose to finance political parties for their own ends. This creates the situation of government of the people by vested interest and lobbying rather than in the best interests of the majority of the population. In the USA this is completely endemic owing to their extraordinary elaborate drawn out and colossally expensive electoral process.

The solution to this is essentially quite straightforward, political parties should be financed by the state, not by private donation. This will at a stroke eliminate the power of financial lobbying and the manipulation of politics by powerful vested interests. I am not going to speculate just exactly how this could be done as it is the effective wisdom principle that is important here. The main point is that it should be entirely illegal for any politician or political party to accept any private financial backing whatsoever. The argument that is put forward is that the public would never agree to public money being given up to support the political process, but the opportunity cost to society far outweighs the financial cost of such a provision. The enhancement in the integrity of the whole process is well worth the cost.

We do however need to develop this a little further, even if we ensure that there is no corruption of the political process through the financing by special interests. We have still not avoided the problem of the disproportionate infestation of our political parties by our dear self-interested friends the capital addicts. Remember, you cannot serve both mammon and the path to wisdom and therefore it is a virtual certainty that Government by the disproportionately wealthy will not be wise in the context of the needs of the many.

Remember our speculation on multiples earlier? I shall, recap to refresh our memories; this was the concept that the maximum acceptable level of personal resource extraction from society could be judged as a multiple of the average. I speculated on a figure of a multiple of 15 which would mean in the UK at this time about £1.75 million. What I am now proposing as part of our wise parliament that nobody who had personal assets above this figure would be allowed to stand for parliamentary election. What is more, they would have to immediately resign if they were found to have exceeded this figure. This would exclude many of the current incumbents who reside in the current UK Parliament and in particular the current Government Cabinet. Yes I know that this may be hard to quantify and implement but during our current discourse I am looking at the principle of the thing, not the detail. This would immediately exclude everyone in society, harbouring an unhealthy attachment within their id to the lure of mammon, from being able to directly influence the formation of political policy. They would still try to blackmail the Government, threatening to take their money overseas or move their businesses to create unemployment and additional hardship. The attachment to the object of their desires is far more powerful to these poor souls than any feelings of collective responsibility. This is really quite a shame as I am convinced that this would be a path that would offer them far more contentment than further material trappings.

Implementation of both these policies would remove the influence of vested interests and the participation by the excessively greedy at a stroke. When the fortunes of the few are intrinsically tied into the fortunes of the many you have created a healthier environment for the development of a wise Government. Yes I know that both of these proposals are a restriction on the personal freedom to indulge oneself, but the benefit to the many will far outweigh the limitations to the self-interest of the few. We could go further than this; if we use the teachings of the wisdom teachers as our guide we know that attachment to greed and self-interest is not even to the personal benefit of these sad capital addicts from the perspective of internal reason and harmony. Naturally they are unlikely to have any comprehension of this in the firm belief that feeding the appetite of their attachment creates meaning and purpose in their lives rather than a rather perverse form of slavery to the demands of HAB. So endemic is the attachment to greed in our society and within these sad souls that any criticism of their right to hoard unlimited amounts of personal wealth is actually referred to as "the politics of envy." They believe that all of my species genuinely desire to also waste their lives chasing ever larger pots of gold and wondering why we still feel that something is intrinsically missing in our lives. It's like having a vast appetite at a never ending feast where no matter how much a person consumes, they never feel full or satisfied. This becomes far from rewarding after a while, but they still cannot escape the pangs of hunger and if they stop eating, these hunger pangs immediately intensify. Not a whole lot to be envious about really, no enlightened and compassionate human would wish such an affliction on another and this is why the wisdom traditions spend so much time warning people against such a path. I don't think the writers of the Bhagavad Gita were engaged in the politics of envy do you?

ORB:- Ok Buzzard, as we are still speculating, how could you create an alternative sense of purpose for the capital addicts amongst us rather than chasing yet more resources to feed their addiction? What alternatives could you provide in the event that you could actually pass legislation to limit their greedy obsessions?

Well this is very theoretical because they would employ every bit of influence they had through coercion, fear and threats to prevent such a society from ever coming into being but I take up your kind offer to continue to speculate.

So let's say that we have actually managed to get a parliament elected that is not addicted to capital owing to the cap we have placed on eligibility, and that they have managed to pass laws on wage and capital multiples. We'll use the figures we have already come up with although I continue to stress that these are purely illustrative and certainly not optimal. Deriving optimal multiples would require much more study. In our example we are now in a situation where it is illegal to hoard more than 15 times the average capital achieved within a given society and not earn more than 10 times the average salary in any given organisation.

The first thing that will happen is that everyone who has capital exceeding this figure would scream with indignation and immediately threaten to leave the country taking their wealth with them.

ORB:- This is one of the threats you have spoken of?

Indeed! To be more kind a compassionate government may be inclined to phase in any such legislation over a period of say 5 years to enable people to adjust. This is however usually the very first threat used by organisations and individuals if any Government threatens to take unilateral action against greed. This is why so many Governments in my world are largely ineffective and feel powerless while the capital addicts feel that they have their hands firmly on the levers of power. I actually believe however that this would have far less impact than we may fear because most of this capital is not being invested for the common good or in the institutions of state but is being hoarded and hived off to tax havens where it is actually pretty useless from the point of view of wider society. It would be amazing if we could suddenly collectively alter the psyches of these sad humans so that they unilaterally decided to re-invest all this money back for the benefit of employees, customers, charities, education, social services, health and welfare. Alas this is a ridiculous fantasy. Don't forget they will already claim that they do this through this strange notion of trickledown of benefits that we have already discussed, and which the current economic devastation categorically proves to be an elaborate myth.

In an ideal scenario, every country in the world would enact the same legislation and insist that surplus capital was returned to and reinvested in the societies that actually created the wealth and therefore enabled it to be extracted in the first place. This would create a world where there was indeed no place to run to and in which, kicking and screaming the capital addicts of the world would have to face up to the nature of their addiction. This is extremely unlikely to happen because we know that Governments around the world are full of the self-same worshipers of mammon who would be only too delighted to offer a home to kindred spirits. Naturally some of the assets of these individuals could be frozen and retained but this would be very difficult to achieve in a global financial marketplace. What the country would is point out that it would be a one way ticket because the choice made by these sad souls to personally own capital above the prescribed limit would be a criminal offence. These individuals would not be able to return without facing massive fines to bring them within the acceptable limits and/or a spell in prison where their addiction could be treated.

Any country implementing such a legislative process would go through enormous financial and civil turmoil as it adjusted to a culture that seems completely alien and incomprehensible living in the one we have today. I do however believe that the society that would emerge from this would be a very positive place to live and a much more harmonious one with a very different set of values. I also feel that those who have previously been fixated by the lure of material acquisition might actually find a much more rewarding purpose to their lives.

ORB: Such as?

Well let's not forget that many of these people are highly intelligent, if not actually wise owing to their lack of essence, and have a range of skills that could be of huge benefit to the societies in which they live. Having achieved considerable personal wealth by reaching the acceptable cap defined by the democratic process there now comes the question of what do they do now? Traditionally the only motive for these people is to apply their skills to accumulate even more wealth but as we have discussed this is largely a pointless exercise bringing scant intrinsic reward to these individuals. Now they could go on massive spending sprees on themselves, ensuring that in each year they buy large amounts of consumables that can feed their hedonistic desires without accumulating any additional capital and that is fine as it goes. Although this would do little to enhance their personal wellbeing it would at least re-cycle this wealth back into the goods and service providers meeting the needs of this appetite. The other thing they could do is use their skills to continue to develop capital and services, not for themselves, but for the other humans who they share society with. Highly skilled businesspeople can still sit on the boards of companies to create wealth, but if they are already "maxed out" in their existing wealth they could do this purely for the benefit of others and of course their own psyche. Rather than personally owning more and more shares they can distribute these to the employees who are committed to the business. Decisions in business would be made on the basis of how an organisation could best enhance the wellbeing of the employees that work there, ensure that the needs of customers are a driving focus to maintain a competitive advantage for the benefit of the many, and also be far more focused on the needs of society. What would not happen is that the boardrooms of corporations and financial institutions would continue to be seen as a vehicle for creating ever increasing amounts of personal wealth to feed the capital addiction of the incumbents. There would just be no point.

ORB:- Wouldn't you lose many of those who already reside in these places who, on the basis of the huge escalations in salaries and bonuses are extremely unlikely to be motivated by anything other than their addiction? What about the skills drain that would ensue?

This comes to the crux of the matter. If you are an employee, shareholder or customer, the last thing you want are capital addicts firmly embedded within the boardroom, just like it is desirable to prevent them holding the levers of political power. A capital addict will always default to feeding the cravings of their addiction and material self-advancement, it will colour every judgement they make. This is why the stock markets over the last 30 years have grown so pitifully whilst the amount of money extracted to tax havens has exploded. As an aside I would advise anyone interested in just how much wealth has been extracted from our societies by these people to read the book "Treasure Islands" by Nicholas Shaxson, a truly an alarming read. It is not even that many of these people are deliberately causing wider harm or even knowingly believe they are feeding their addiction; many of them will genuinely believe that they are acting in the public good. With no understanding of the power of HAB and its imperatives driven from their unconscious, they are in many cases probably blissfully unaware of how their decisions are being shaped by their own unconscious psyche. Once the attachment is firmly established on greed and material acquisition the rest is just an inevitable, almost mechanical consequence.

The new model of corporate governance I am proposing where companies are run for the benefit of society and employees is not new or original to this discourse. There is a group of people with a highly developed sense of essence and therefore great wisdom called the Quakers who are amongst the most Jesian of the Christian groups I have come across. Many famous names in banking and industry originated through such groups but alas most of these are now in the hands of the capital addicts. It is sad that such people seem to be less influential in the corporate sphere than they once were which I believe is a great loss to society.

One of the very saddest examples of this which shows just how much wisdom can be eroded is one of the most famous banks that originated as a Quaker organisation. This bank now has a money making investment function that actually speculates on the value of essential food produce around the world which has the perverse function of raising the price of food to feed the hunger of their capital addiction. This is causing millions of the most vulnerable and impoverished of the peoples of the world to suffer malnutrition and die of related diseases, particularly the children whose parents can no longer afford to feed them. The Quakers who created this bank would be absolutely horrified to see such practices going on in our so called developed society. Making profit at the expense of the lives of others, profit from death, is however entirely legal and has the implicit support of our Governments. You see what can happen when you get Capital addicts in the boardroom? Yes, making large sums of money by speculating of basic food commodities is undoubtedly clever but it is the polar opposite of wisdom. As we have said so many times before, using information without essence can never produce wise outcomes.

ORB:- You have mentioned the opportunity cost of hoarding capital on a number of occasions. What do you mean by this?

Ok, let us look at a multi-millionaire who may own several very expensive cars, a luxury yacht or two and probably two or three houses dotted around. At the same time there are fellow humans sharing their society where whole families are sharing one room and who may even struggle to get food on the table. Our streets are home to many of our most vulnerable, many with mental health conditions and whose life expectancy may be just half of that of our dear affluent capital hoarder. The price of the extra BMW or the houses that they don't need or the luxury yacht that they may only use a few weeks a year could transform the lives of dozens of their fellow humans. Rather than extracting it, directing this wealth to lower paid employees or contributing this surplus to charities such as Centre Point for the homeless would make a huge difference to the lives of others.

There are other, less obvious ways that excessive greed can have a dramatic negative impact on the wellbeing of others. The salaries and bumper bonuses in the City of London and the attraction of highly favourable tax regulations for foreign nationals has created a huge housing price bubble in London. This has dragged up the price of housing to the extent that even many of the key workers required to keep London's services going have been driven out to the suburbs and beyond. There are now huge waiting lists for social housing which would be entirely unnecessary if excessive wealth had been capped and re-invested into society instead.

Even the strange game of football has suffered. The only way the large clubs can survive and successfully compete is by being bought as a plaything by those multi-millionaires or in a number of cases, billionaires who are bored with their lives and need a distraction. They have bought successful teams by paying millions of pounds for vainglorious players to fill their ranks making it virtually impossible for any club without a capital addict pay-rolling them to compete.

This has not benefitted football in the least. It is now utterly boringly predictable as everyone knows that the Premier League will always be won by one of a handful of clubs with super rich patrons. Other clubs are going bankrupt trying to pay wage bills to attract players on hugely inflated salaries owing to the over hyped market created by these wealthy owners. Just imagine what the game would be like without all these bored tycoons? Players' salaries would be a fraction of what they are now and they would actually play for the passion of the game rather than the passion of their bank balances. Ticket prices would be readily affordable to the fans, any team with a good manager would stand a chance of winning, and the game of football would actually become unpredictable and exciting.

My species has arrived at the state when it is considered perfectly acceptable for individuals to accumulate vast amounts of resources at the expense of the rest of society. It is an utter mystery to me how these humans, many of whom to all intents and purposes seem on the surface to be rational and kindly people can think that their second or third house is more important than a homeless family. The usual arguments are that they do their bit by paying taxes or that everyone else has a chance to be a capital addict too and it is their own fault if they are poor. These are truly pitiful and hollow rationalisations that their egos use to justify succumbing to the perverse attachment they have through their HAB to greed. Now we have already said that some accumulation of capital can be beneficial but we know that individuals virtually never constrain this behaviour through their own volition to a sensible point beyond which it becomes grotesque. This is why it is so important that a majority consensus for an acceptable limit is defined by society and that the wealth generated by the collective effort of society is recycled for the benefit of the majority not just the few.

ORB:- *So why would these people continue to contribute to society when they have reached the maximum allowable capital?*

Well they don't have to. They can resign from their corporations or live off their substantial permissible savings should they choose to do so, this will allow others who are building their careers to take over their jobs and create new healthy competition in the boardroom marketplace. Like the footballer scenario, you may also start to attract people who are actually motivated by the job and developing organisations for the benefit of customers, shareholders, employees and wider society rather than feeding their addiction to personal greed. I am completely convinced that these corporations, financial institutions and public organisations would really start to flourish in such circumstances. This will be to the benefit of all society.

Alternatively, should those previously addicted to acquiring personal capital continue to acquire capital for the benefit of wider society, this could bring enormous emotional reward. Imagine having a successful business person in your local community who has "maxed out" on their allowed personal capital but who continues to earn more than they consume and contributes to society by ploughing the excess back to support the community? Imagine that this money, rather than buying yet another expensive car or an even bigger yacht that they don't remotely need was instead used to build new classrooms for the local school, new equipment for the local hospital or subsidising transport for the elderly and the infirm? This would have transformational effects within the community and rather than being an object of sadness and derision as they currently deserve, they would become a person to celebrate and admire. I am absolutely convinced that by applying their skills and resources for the benefits of others in their community these humans would find their lives so much more rewarding. Attachment and service to the wellbeing of others will bring these people so much more happiness than their current obsession with capital acquisition and personal greed. This would indeed be the planting of a seed of wisdom and start an important internal journey of self-enquiry as to their true purpose and the positive potential of a human existence.

ORB:- It is interesting that you recommended that people maxed out on their capital allowance could use their skills for the benefit of the local community, why not nationally or internationally?

Well they could do this. This would be equally positive but I think that their HAB may be more likely to create attachments to a local community who they could become directly involved with and share in the benefits provided to all. This is often the problem with general taxation policies that the wealthiest always seem to rail so much against. It is just an unemotional bureaucratic bucket whose output, although vital for the existence and functionality of the nation, is difficult to perceive and is unlikely to be an attractive object for the properties of HAB. This is one explanation that capital addicts often employ to rationalise their greed as they assert that if they hand over money to the Government they will just waste it. Even the most incompetent Government is unlikely to waste it on something as meaningless as adding another million to an already overflowing pot but this is the point; HAB is not rational. The default position of exceeding the capital wealth limit would be to lose the excess to national taxation but this would not use HAB to create the most positive advantage for the wider community. As I have alluded to, HAB need not always be a handicap if its properties are well understood and managed. HAB can be utilised to create a wider harmony instead of the normal disharmony that seems to arise from the attachments it makes.

There is a dynamic here that is interesting; a person can have a very substantial impact if they apply themselves to their local community or charitable cause, a marginal one if applied to a district or county issue and make virtually no identifiable difference if applied to a national issue. The initiation of this outward looking philosophy for the benefit of the wider community locally can also be positively driven up the chain. This is one of the most fundamental transformations that needs to take place if our poor species is ever to further evolve rather than regress. It is changing the perspective from focusing on one's own material (not to be confused with cognitive) gain in direct competition with, and often at the expense of others. We need the wisdom and through wisdom, the realisation that each one of us is genuinely more secure and liberated if we focus on how we can help others. Remember the metaphor with the Hoplite and the Phalanx? Again this is an absolute foundation of the wisdom traditions, not out of any pious sentiment towards doing good, but through the realisation that this is in a person's genuine self-interest, directly contributing to the development of a more harmonious psyche. Focusing on how we can be of service to others and create a more harmonious world starves our id and ego-ideal of fuel for the most damaging and destructive self-focused attachments that cause so much internal and external disharmony. If we can achieve this perspective as individuals and develop our communities upon this basis, our institutions and communities will also start to look outwards.

Using this philosophical approach, as well as looking after the needs of the local community our local groups and councils would actively start to look at the contribution they could make in the interests of wider society. I can remember with sad resignation the Prime Minister of my country coming back from a meeting with 26 other members of the European Community saying that he had vetoed a motion as it was not in our national interest. As an aside, this motion was to protect society from the institutions representing the very worst viral capitalists in our financial sector from outside regulation. The painful fact that these institutions had just successfully fleeced the people of my country out of many £billions didn't help my humour. The bigger point however is that compromising self-interest or even national interest to create a greater harmony is actually in everyone's best interest. The eventual rewards of such an approach for creating a more supportive and harmonious world will ultimately far outweigh any short term selfish gain. It is such a transformation in the perspective of my species and our collective psyche that would be the most conspicuous evidence that we had returned to a path of rational evolution.

From this perspective let's speculate on how the individual dynamic of service to the local community could migrate through the layers of Government and society. The application of additional resources and revenues at local or parish level can enable the local people and their council to look at making a greater contribution for the funding of additional services that would be supplied by a district or county council. Equally, the county councils can be looking to make an enhanced contribution to the wellbeing of national initiatives such as road and rail infrastructure or scientific enquiry or new sources of energy. If the nations of the world are benefiting from all this new recycled investment within their communities, they can focus more on the welfare of international efforts and directives. Great international projects for the benefits of all of humanity can be supported. Examples of these are the existing Large Hadron Collider that is unlocking the secrets of the universe or the space telescopes. Humanity could look to the further development of nuclear fusion technology which holds the promise of virtually unlimited energy without polluting radioactive waste. More importantly, humanity needs to urgently adopt a global responsibility for stopping the widespread destruction to the environment and the other beings that share our planet.

It is a great tragedy that decades of focus on creating wealth through unregulated and unconstrained markets, utterly ignoring the attachments and self-interest of the players within them, has led to virtual bankruptcy of national and international bodies. I can remember the incredible joy that I felt as a young person when the first human stood on the moon in 1969. I think we all thought that it would be a mere matter of a couple of decades before a human was standing on the planet Mars and yet 43 years later this goal seems further away than ever. The wealth that could have been channelled into such awe inspiring projects to increase our understanding of the world and the universe is pointlessly sat in the bank accounts of various sad capital addicts to feed their HAB induced addiction. Many great projects for the collective interest of humanity are being cut back or cancelled because there is no money left to finance them. How is it in these 43 years since the first moon landing that collectively humanity is more impoverished today than it was all those years ago? The answer is sadly that we have allowed our collective psyche as a species to become so infected with the viruses of self-interest, greed and intolerance of others that we are now on the verge of not just the collapse of our societies but also irreparable damage to our planet. The current generation's focus on its own selfish desires is destroying the prospects for all the generations to come and ignoring our responsibility to the other beings on this planet who are suffering so much at our hands. We have created a selfish, ignorant and angry world; there has never been a greater need for the collective application of wisdom based values and never such little evidence of any dynamic towards this goal.

Chapter 11 - The threat to our planet and the relevance of wisdom for a sustainable future

ORB:- You have mentioned on a number of occasions the threat that your species poses to your planet. You make your species sound like one of these viral infections that eventually kills off the host that is needed for its own survival. As we have come to expect from your species, this does not seem to be a very rational approach. Please elaborate on these concerns for me and continue in the spirit of speculation as to how this dynamic could be reversed?

The sad truth is that this focus on self-interest rather than collective interest is creating an unsustainable dynamic. The constant refrain from politicians is the generation of economic growth rather than economic and environmental sustainability. We actually produce and squander as a species far more than we need. A good indicator of this is if we look at the emissions of a gas called Carbon Dioxide or CO2 per person on the planet. This is produced through the burning of hydrocarbons such as oil, coal and gas to produce energy. If we look at comparably developed countries such as the United States of America and the United Kingdom and Germany we find that the average production of CO2 per capita in the USA (2009 figures) is approximately 17.7 tonnes whilst in the UK it is 8.3 tonnes and in Germany, a highly industrialised manufacturing country, 9.3 tonnes. This is a good indicator of just how much energy is wasted in the USA and I know as a resident of the UK that we still have a very wasteful society. The most worrying thing is that the global average is just 4.5 tonnes but as many of the previously underdeveloped nations in the world evolve economically this figure will rapidly grow.

There are two fundamental problems here, if countries continue to evolve on the basis of the viral capitalist model then the consumption of the world's resources and the destruction of the environment will become unsustainable. Already in many countries the lakes and rivers have become poisoned and, despite those in denial usually at the behest of corporate interests, the world's climate is changing. This will lead to increased desertification in many areas whilst at the same time the world's stocks of fresh water are becoming rapidly depleted under pressure of population explosion and industrialisation. The fish stocks in the world's oceans are now under so much intense pressure owing to demands made upon them through human consumption that many species have completely collapsed and may never recover. In short the current human approach to consumption is unsustainable.

This is all compounded by an even bigger problem which is the explosion of the human population on the planet, the metaphor with a virus that ultimately destroys its host is not that far removed from the truth. Since 1960 the world's population has more than doubled from 3 billion to 7 billion in 2012 and at current rates of growth this will reach at least 10 billion by 2050. The cost to our planet of supporting such a population, particularly if economic activity continues to increase is likely to be truly cataclysmic. This is likely to lead to mass starvation, wars over scarce resources and the mass destruction of other planetary beings as a minimum. The tensions created by the fight for resources could even lead to the ultimate catastrophe of nuclear conflict. The unrestrained viral capitalist model for the future of the species will therefore lead to the destruction of all. This sad situation is not helped by the fact that many religions including the Godotian based ones simultaneously rail against attempts at reducing the incidence of births through any attempt at contraception or active birth control measures. Apparently it's all part of Godot's master plan!

Rather strangely from my perspective in a western democratic country, I look with tremendous admiration to the People's Republic of China. At huge individual cost but for the collective benefit of the Chinese people and the wider population of the world they implemented a policy of restricting much of the population to having only 1 child and virtually all the rest for having no more than 2. This has, as estimated from Chinese Government sources, prevented over 400 million births since it was introduced in 1979. The environmental and economic benefits in a country that is rapidly developing have already been felt and will become even more apparent as the population eventually peaks and starts to decline, predicted to happen in 2030 or near about.

In most economically developed countries populations have stabilised but in underdeveloped countries or in countries where this economic development is in transition the populations continue to explode. Even if these countries adopted policies like China's now, based on the Chinese model it will take 60 years for the population growth in these areas to peak. The advantage that China had is that it did not have the much cherished democratic system of Government but had a one party centralised Government model that could effectively impose constraint on the population. It is difficult to see how this could be done in democratic countries where politicians have to get elected through the popular vote. This is the absolute dilemma for my species; wisdom implies that the human population needs to be limited for the benefit of all but self-interest leads many people to have numerous children. This is often linked to poverty. In poor societies the adult population have well founded anxieties about who will look after them as they grow older. The historically high incidence of child mortality in these societies spur them on to have large families to ensure that sufficient children survive into adulthood. With the advent of modern healthcare and vaccination programmes many of the diseases that used to limit these populations are now being eradicated so levels of childhood mortality are falling away. The result of this is a population explosion that can be equally as traumatic as some of the historical diseases as supplies of water and food come under increasing pressure from growing populations resulting in malnutrition and starvation. As previously stated, the problem of unconstrained population growth is often compounded by cultural and religious imperatives that encourage this practice.

The imposed self-discipline on population control by China is also a model for the discipline required to rein in greed and the excesses of capital addiction. Just as many of the people of China would have dearly liked to have more children, so individuals in our greed based model of society would also wish to have an unrestricted right to extract disproportionately high resources from a limited resource pool. They will not exercise self-control voluntarily but do our societies have the potential maturity to impose constraints? As mentioned so many times, I fear that they do not and so the majority will continue to support a model for society that celebrates excessive greed and which actively harms this same complicit majority. To use a truly relevant saying, we collectively shoot ourselves in the foot.

I am not saying that I believe the Chinese model of Government is necessary in order to impose policies that inhibit self-interest and choice for the collective good. It certainly makes this process so much easier but much of the world, including my country has firmly adopted a model of democratic government. The peoples of these countries are extremely unlikely to give up this form of government for a more totalitarian regime except under conditions of severe threat and hardship. The rise of the dictatorships in Germany, Spain and Italy after the great recession of the 1930s does however show that this is by no means inevitable. The solution is therefore far more challenging because I have no doubt for the need to rein in the excesses caused by HAB in our societies but this will have to come from a popular mandate. Any momentum towards building this mandate will be actively resisted by the forces of viral capitalism that control virtually all the current leavers of power; the corporations, financial institutions, media outlets and of course many of our most influential politicians.

ORB:- So how could you envisage this happening?

As stated many times before, I don't envisage it happening; I sadly believe that my species may be beyond any help owing to the very nature of the human psyche. Thousands of years of wisdom teaching appear to have had virtually no impact upon humanity. This is evidenced by its attachments to fear based religious doctrines and its obsessions with greed and self-interest resulting in frequent manifestations of fear, insecurity, guilt, self-loathing and anger. I think the result of this, as previously discussed, is the nature of many of the objects of attachment initiated through HAB. Any hope of significant change will be through providing alternative more positive objects as an attraction to the properties of HAB, ones that promote both inner and collective harmony. This is indeed a tall order.

It is not however impossible as we have previously mentioned, my species can in the right environment and with positive role models also display extraordinary generosity and kindness. What is even more important, these characteristics also make humans feel much more in harmony and at peace within themselves. This is actually a very good starting point for any of my species who, like me, struggle to relate to the obvious absurdities so evident in human society. It may be incredibly unlikely that we can change society but we can all work to change ourselves and, if enough people undertake this path, this will inevitably start to influence the societies in which they live. This is very much a Buddhist perspective, if you want the world to change this has to start with change within oneself. It is difficult to conceive the possibility of making a wise world without at least attempting to gain an element of personal wisdom. I do however believe that time is running out for my species and with it any lingering hopes of changing the current dynamic within much of global society that is contributing to the regression rather than evolution of my species. Developing an evolutionary path towards wisdom inspired evolution will therefore require a more proactive attitude. It is in this respect that the peculiar properties of HAB can actually come to our service should we allow ourselves to become emotionally attached to the concept of creating a wise and compassionate society.

I do have some further advice to offer anyone of my species who does decide to act to influence the human world, this will be a long and frustrating business and therefore it is necessary to focus on positive intent rather than outcome. As Sri Krishnan says to Arjuna in the Bhagavad Gita; *"You have the right to work, but never engage in action for the sake of reward, nor should you long for inaction. Perform work in this world Arjuna, as a man established within himself- without selfish attachments, and alike in success and defeat."* These are wise words for everyone who feels that we all have an obligation to try to make the world a more harmonious place and take our responsibilities as custodians of our planet seriously. Always be guided by positive intent as the path to change will always be a rocky one and will be met by many setbacks.

ORB:- You have mentioned this concept of a wise society and have stated that it is necessary for those who are passionate about this concept to act but I feel it would be helpful if, from your perspective you could clarify what you believe a wise society would look like?

I feel somewhat uncomfortable about answering this as I believe that this is a question that should be answered by those more enlightened than myself. Defining the characteristics of a wise society requires collective dialogue from many rational voices to forge its defining terms. I will however express a personal view in the realisation of the limitations of such an approach.

Most importantly it is necessary to consider the concepts of harmony and disharmony and understand that a wise society evolves both by the development of the individual human psyches of those within it, and in the structures and guidelines used to coordinate human activity in a harmonious way.

If we are to strive towards creating a harmonious society we have to each understand our personal obligations and act out of a sense of responsibility. Thi applies to our responsibility towards to other humans and the other types of being who share our world and suffer so badly at our hands. It also applies with regard to our obligations as the custodians of our fragile world on behalf of the generations to come. Some points that I believe may be helpful in this regard are listed below.

1. We are all subject to HAB and it is extraordinarily difficult for the cognitive part of our consciousness to escape from the unconscious attachments that are made without any conscious desire on our part. Ignoring HAB is futile and rather than get annoyed with other humans for illogical attachments we should show understanding and compassion. We should all strive to engage with others with due humility in the knowledge that each of us is also largely a slave to the manipulations of HAB.

2. Understanding the nature of HAB, a wise society would offer positive objects of attachment worthy of the human spirit. Worthy objects and ideas for attachment are the protection and support of the vulnerable in our species and others, and a celebration and consequent responsibility to the incredible world we live on and the universe in which it is embedded.

3. Wisdom is comprised of information and knowledge in the context of essence. A wise society will also need to create an essence that is based on collective responsibility, equality and fairness not individual advantage and greed. A wise society will be primarily based on our responsibilities to each other and the beings and world around us. Defining a society on the basis of self-interest and greed is guaranteed to create wider disharmony, strife, increased inequality and injustice. In a wise society people will be admired for how they look out for the needs of others rather than celebrated on how they feed their own selfish desires and appetites.

4. Humanity needs to recognise that, in a world of limited resources, we should all be minded to take only that which we need. This is a philosophical point so an acceptable upper limit needs to be defined and enforced by society although the wiser amongst us may choose a more conservative level of acquisition. The last 30 years have proved without doubt that those cursed with an addiction to material wealth by the properties of HAB are not in control of their capital addiction and indeed lack the rationality to constrain themselves. There are now, despite the incredible indebtedness of much of the world's people and their nations, more billionaires than ever before. Inequality is increasing in virtually every society on the planet. This dynamic will not stop itself, it will require external control.

5. In parliamentary democracies you will not constrain the manipulation of society by the avaricious and greedy unless political parties are publically funded so they cannot be controlled by vested interests. It is also essential that capital addicts are prohibited from holding office as they cannot but help their unconscious, yet incredibly powerful attachment to material wealth, influencing every decision they make. The selfish and greedy are not those who will develop a wisdom based society.

6. Public services such as education and health will be better for all if all are required to use them. Allowing the most advantaged to source specific privilege in these areas is guaranteed to see a deterioration of service quality for the majority. A harmonious society cannot ignore the impact on

the majority by the selfish actions of the few, and no remotely enlightened being would wish it to be any other way.

7. You cannot build a harmonious and tolerant world based on the inspiration of Godot type Gods conceived with the worst of human frailties. This concept of God, as defined by the religious texts of the principle God faiths is angry, vengeful, narcissistic, intolerant, cruel, and utterly contemptible of human life and suffering. This concept of a God offers the polar opposite to wisdom and is a woefully inadequate representation of the beauty and harmony of the Unot. How can a creative force behind the universe and all within it, be realised through an entity that shows every possible weakness of the most impoverished and underdeveloped of human psyches? If this is your inspiration then this will also be the nature of the society you will build I will say no more on this subject except to encourage people to look at societies that follow such doctrines and ask if they have served humanity well?

8. In a world of over 7 billion people, harsh but fair choices have to be made on how many children a human can responsibly be allowed to have. This is a tough ask but failure to act will destroy our world and lead to strife, hardship conflict and ultimately terrible suffering and death for millions. The people of China, at great personal cost, have shown the world an admirable sense of responsibility that we all need to follow if we are to create a sustainable world. You cannot develop a harmonious world that is unsustainable. Unfortunately parents in many societies, like my own, have no sanction on how many offspring they have and have little regard as to who will actually end up trying to support their children. A wiser world has to be built on a sense of individual responsibility and unfortunately societies will have to take sanctions against those who consistently act in their own self-interests at the expense of others. A responsible society requires those within it to also act responsibly.

9. Lastly, I would encourage every human to look for inspiration from the teachings of the wisdom traditions. Of course a personal delight in this

regard would be the development of a Jesian movement that casts off the burden of Godot. Understanding and come to terms with the nature of the Unot by freeing oneself from the constraints imposed by HAB can offer a path towards inner peace and harmony for troubled minds. The great thing about following a wisdom path is that it is also entirely compatible with revelations from science; it just approaches the Unot from a different perspective. Anyone who has strived to develop an inner harmony cannot but promote a wider harmony in the society and the world around them.

So ORB, there you have it, this is my personal take on the nature of a wise society but my strong caveat to this is that there are much wiser heads than mine on this planet who should be encouraged to wrestle with this subject. I also think that this should be the prerogative of the younger generation not an old cynic like the Buzzard. It is the young who are inheriting the global mess we have created for them and unfortunately we have to pass the burden of responsibility for change onto their shoulders. They have the opportunity to develop a very different world should they choose to do so but this will take an extraordinary effort and the evolution of a determined and collective will if they are to achieve this. This is a possibility through the democratic process, but they will have to wrest the levers of power and control from those who wish to hold on to these for their own self-interests and manipulations. Alas, the attractions and attachments of HAB that have led my generation and many generations before to so spectacularly fail are just as strong in the psyches of today's young humans as they were in ours. I fear that there may indeed be no escape for my poor species with predictably dire consequences for all humanity and the other species that also share our beautiful and fragile planet.

ORB:- *Thank you Buzzard for an intriguing, if somewhat perplexing dialogue. I truly fear for your poor species and like you feel that there is but a slender hope for their evolution towards a more rational and sustainable future. Do you have any last comment to make before we go our separate ways?*

I can do no better than to refresh the mind with a couple of the quotes from Jesus as recorded in the Gospel of Thomas;

94. Jesus said, "One who seeks will find, and for one who knocks it will be opened."

113. His disciples said to him, "When will the kingdom come?"

"It will not come by watching for it. It will not be said, 'Look, here!' or 'Look, there!' Rather, the Father's kingdom is spread out upon the earth, and people don't see it."

Made in the USA
Charleston, SC
17 September 2016